The Write Stuff Adventure

Exploring the Art of Writing

Dean Rea

GREAT EXPECTATIONS
BOOK CO.

The Write Stuff Adventure

Copyright © 1999 by Dean Rea
Published by Great Expectations Book Company
P.O. Box 2067 • Eugene, Oregon 97402

ISBN 1-883934-04-4

Printed in the United States of America.

04 05 06 07 08 09 10 / 15 14 13 12 11 10 9 8 7 6 5 4

Contents

Foreword by Duncan McDonald
Introduction

Section One: Simple Things

Section Two: Personal and Family History

Section Three: The Essay Made Easy

Section Four: Interviewing and the Non-Fiction Article

Acknowledgments

My greatest inspiration for this book originated with the home school students who wrote, rewrote and wrote again while we shared our thoughts, our lives and our dreams during *The Write Stuff Adventure*.

Without the cheerleading and editing help of my wife, Lou, this book would not have materialized. When I began searching for a book topic, she wisely suggested: "You've been teaching writing to home school students. Why not write about that?"

Parents of home school students contributed greatly to this enterprise by critiquing assignments and by encouraging their students during our exploration.

LuAnn Rea, a daughter-in-law and home school teacher, was my associate in mapping out this instructional program. Without her guidance, this adventure would not have materialized.

Cheri Reinhard's critique of *Write Stuff* lessons that she used in teaching a group of home school students proved invaluable.

Others who advised and encouraged me in this endeavor include authors Linda Shands, Bob Welch, David Kopp, Ken Metzler, Roy Paul Nelson, William "Bill" Sullivan, Elizabeth Lyon and Duncan McDonald.

Dedication

To Jaime Lyn and Stephanie,
two granddaughters who accompanied me on
The Write Stuff Adventure.

Foreword
By Duncan McDonald

My old friend and colleague Dean Rea has it right, as usual—writing is indeed an "adventure." He's a pretty good salesman, too, as I am confident that home-schooled students will be attracted to "The Write Stuff Adventure" for all the right reasons.

Professor Rea (if I can hearken back to his University of Oregon days) has authored a comprehensive and thoughtful guide to writing instruction that has much to offer both teacher and student. His curriculum is well-paced and builds on a sensible foundation that encourages self-paced growth.

As someone who has spent most of his professional career as both writer and teacher, I must applaud Rea's encouragement of creative writing through easy-to-understand assignments that provide important building blocks. His assignments often have more than one purpose: In Lesson 12 of his first section (Simple Things), he makes understanding the role of prepositions and prepositional phrases easy—and fun. How? Find out in "The Rabbit Drill."

Rea's curriculum and assignments build to longer-form challenges, including the short story. (I suspect that the curious student will look ahead to future assignments and even do some out of order. That may provide helpful clues to the home-school teacher: to add more assignments of a similar ilk once a student offers such a clue.)

The teaching of writing has often been viewed as an impossible task. Some pessimists even argue that "writers are born, not made." I dissent, and my proof will be the results of Rea's efforts. A well-structured, nicely placed curriculum that provides both reward and critical feedback does work. And it is work well worth doing because many of our educational institutions are, sad to say, failing in their responsibility to provide structured but creative programs for improving communication skills. This is not the place to replay the "Whole Language" debate, so suffice to say that *The Write Stuff Adventure* shows that writing based on high expectations of both proper form and compelling, coherent content can be taught, learned and practiced with flourish.

Many thanks, Dean Rea! You've performed an important service to education. I'm grateful to you for proving that good teachers never stop teaching.

Duncan McDonald is the former dean of the School of Journalism and Communication and is now vice president of Public Affairs and Development at the University of Oregon in Eugene.

Introduction

After my retirement from full-time teaching, I volunteered to work with two granddaughters who were being home schooled. The girls, 10 and 12, had been taught grammar, punctuation and other language skills by their mother. I realized that this would be a unique opportunity to share the information gathering and writing skills that I had acquired during a newspaper and university teaching career that spanned a half century.

Granted, I had never taught elementary or high school students, but I decided that working one-on-one with motivated, intellectually bright and well-behaved granddaughters for an hour or so a week would offer a learning experience for me as well as for the girls. Together, we would explore the craft of writing. As you might expect, we worked hard, laughed together and shed tears on occasion. Through the years, my granddaughters and other students who joined us discovered that writing can be enjoyable and rewarding. That discovery made the adventure worthwhile.

During the first year, I met with each granddaughter for an hour weekly beginning in the fall. I recall that the youngest, who was in the fifth grade, was somewhat reluctant to participate. I knew she was concerned about her writing and spelling skills. So, I suggested that she use a tape recorder to complete the first writing assignment. She appeared relieved and we continued this practice for a couple of weeks.

She then inquired: "Granddad, could I write out my assignments? It takes so much more time to use the tape recorder."

"Certainly," I answered, "and don't worry about your spelling. Write what you want to say and have fun doing it." My granddaughter soon began writing with more confidence and since has written articles that have been published in a church newsletter and in a historical journal.

I counted a more difficult cadence for my eldest granddaughter, who exhibited the gift of written expression from the beginning. She nearly balked, however, midway through our first year of study when I assigned her to interview a photographer and to write a story about his exhibit in a shopping mall. Granted, it was a daunting challenge for a 12-year-old, but my granddaughter completed the assignment at the urging of her home school parents. Later, interviewing became one of her strongest skills in a budding career as a professional writer.

We survived the first year of instruction, and I wondered if other home schoolers would like to participate in what I called *The Write Stuff Adventure*. My granddaughters and other parents endorsed the idea and helped recruit students for two classes that paralleled the ages and writing skills of the girls. I soon discovered that dozens of home school parents wanted help with writing instruction. Most felt unqualified to teach the subject. They were anxious to enroll their sons and daughters in my classes, which I limited to 20 students initially and to a dozen eventually. I volunteered my time and charged a nominal fee to cover the cost of photocopying assignments and supplementary material. A church volunteered the use of a classroom.

I worked three years with the senior group and four years with the junior group. I discovered that most home school teachers had equipped their students with basic language skills. I must confess that many of my home school students possessed a better grasp of grammar, language use and punctuation than some of the university journalism students that I had taught.

My stated goal in the *Write Stuff* instruction was never to help create professional writers. Rather, I encouraged students to become effective communicators in any career field, including that of parenting. As you will note later, students wrote letters to grandmothers, prepared instructions for babysitters, wrote speeches and crafted letters to the editor. We learned how to write an essay, a news story, a feature story, a short story and how to take photographs for the family album.

Some students developed an interest in writing that led to publication of articles in church newsletters, newspapers and magazines. On occasion their work was published as a class project and was shared with family members and friends. All of the students succeeded, in part, because of the assistance and support of their home school teachers. Parents, for example, helped students with assignments and made certain that rewrites were completed on time. These parents served as editors who raised questions about such things as story organization, sentence structure, spelling and the logic of a student's line of reasoning or argumentation. As a result, parents discovered that they often were better equipped to teach writing than they had imagined.

With the graduation of my granddaughters from the *Write Stuff* program, I thought it might be helpful to share what I have learned with other home school teachers by writing this instructional guide. Maybe other grandparents with writing skills will be motivated to use this resource in teaching home school classes. I have offered suggestions about what educators call methodology. I call it: "What has worked for me might work for you." The instruction is organized in six segments and can be introduced as early as the fifth or sixth grade. The writing assignments become more difficult and may be spread out over several years. I found that most high school juniors and seniors are too busy to invest the time needed to continue *The Write Stuff Adventure* by learning how to write fiction. I have, however, included suggestions for how a home school teacher can teach short story writing.

You can begin the instruction at any time during the school year, and you can pick assignments from any of the units that best match the skill level of your student.

Students often respond more positively when instruction is offered in small bites. They also are more likely to learn to write if they are encouraged and if they have fun doing it. Underscore the importance of writing by making it a staple in the student's curriculum. Integrate writing assignments with the study of other subjects and don't despair when your sixth grade son insists on writing about aliens and spaceships. He's writing, and that's what *The Write Stuff Adventure* is all about.

Section One:
Simple Things

Note to Teacher

Children don't write for at least four reasons:

1. It isn't fun.
2. It isn't considered important enough to be included in the curriculum.
3. They can't spell.
4. The home school teacher doesn't feel confident and is hesitant to teach writing.

Teachers can correct this problem in four easy steps:

1. Writing every day.

Pick up a pencil and join the fun. If your student sees you writing and if you share what you have written with your student, writing will become a staple in your daily lives and instructional program. You will become more confident of your writing skills and your ability to teach the subject.

2. Don't get hung up on spelling and language skills.

Home schoolers usually are readers. They pick up the pattern of speech and develop a sense of story. They can check the spelling in what they write later. Don't make the mechanics of writing a "big deal" initially. If you do, expect resistance and an aversion to writing.

3. Make writing an adventure.

You're exploring the universe. Integrate writing into other topics that you are studying. Make writing an ally, a helpmate, a communications vehicle.

An example: The student who is assigned to write about the flute, a musical instrument, probably will base the report on research gleaned from an encyclopedia or from an Internet source. Expect the report to be dull, dull, dull. Expect the student to view the assignment as dull, dull, dull. Ever wonder why students don't enjoy writing? Why not assign the student to write a story about a piece of wood that grows into a flute, one with a personality, a name, a real life. Watch the story and the student blossom. It's called fun.

4. Publish.

Post whatever the student writes on the refrigerator. Photocopy something the student has written and send it to grandparents. Invite the student to read a completed assignment to the family after a meal. Verbal presentations also offer an opportunity to teach public speaking.

Home schoolers begin learning how to write almost as soon as they learn how to speak. During the first four or five years of school, they concentrate on learning parts of speech and grammar and developing other language skills. At this point, they are prepared to begin exercising and developing these skills as writers.

The Write Stuff Adventure is organized to help teachers direct this instruction. Teachers who may have had no formal writing training or experience will find that they are quite capable of critiquing the work of students using this study guide. It's a matter of taking one small step at a time and integrating the study of writing into a home schooler's curriculum.

In this textbook a comma is not used before a conjunction in a series of words or phrases. For example: The flag is red, white and blue. I encourage students to follow that practice because many of the *Write Stuff* exercises are intended for publication in newspapers and magazines, which omit the comma before the conjunction as a matter of style. Some students will be studying a grammar book that requires the comma before the conjunction. In that case, I advise students to follow the grammar book rule while taking a test based on that book, then follow my rule when preparing *Write Stuff* assignments.

The lessons that follow in this first unit of instruction are relatively simple, often fun. Pick them at random or use them in sequence. Study a lesson a week or at whatever pace best fits your instructional program. If a student is involved in a month-long science study, make writing a part of that project.

You can begin this study with your student as early as fifth or sixth grade, depending upon his/her language skills. Several lessons review such things as grammar, sentence structure and other language skills. Other assignments preview more detailed studies of fiction and non-fiction writing. Most home schoolers will continue the study of grammar and spelling. They also should be encouraged to learn how to type as soon as their hands are large enough to span a keyboard. Typing and language skills are basic tools that a writer must master to become an effective communicator.

Present this study as an adventure, something that will require some effort but also something that can be fun.

Fun and Games

Everyone loves to play games. Usually, two or more people are required to play. In those games, someone wins and someone loses. In the following word game, however, you play alone and you are always the winner.

Here's how you play the game. Get a list of words that you are learning to spell or are adding to your vocabulary. Pick a half dozen of these words and write each one on a separate piece of paper. Then fold the pieces of paper and place them in a hat.

Close your eyes and draw a word from the hat. Then write the word as part of a sentence. Continue until you have written sentences for each of the six words.

Now, use the six words as you write a short story. Then share the story with your teacher.

Note to Teacher:

You may wish to join the student in this game by writing your own sentences and story by way of example and encouragement.

Don't, however, dwell on misspelled words or grammar. Make this an enjoyable experience, a game.

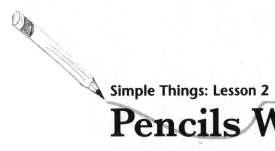

Simple Things: Lesson 2

Pencils Without Erasers

Take a piece of tape and wrap it around the eraser on your pencil.

Now, get a sheet of paper and complete the assignment that follows. If you need to change a word, cross it out and continue writing, but don't erase.

Writers should not be concerned with the hen scratches and changes they make while writing a first draft. They know that changes will be made before a second draft is completed. So, don't waste your time wearing out an eraser.

Assignment:

Write at least 100 words describing what happened to you yesterday. Start with what happened to you in the morning and continue until you went to bed. You can cross out and add words anywhere in your report. Do not erase any words, however.

Show your paper to your teacher.

Note to Teacher:

Point out the things you like about your student's work. Don't dwell on errors. Use this assignment as a tool of encouragement. No rewriting, yet.

Dear Grandmother

You probably have written many letters to your grandmother. Maybe you have thanked her for a Christmas gift. Maybe you have told her about something special that happened to you.

Let's write another letter. Tell her about your summer. What was special about it?

Follow the example below. You can place a comma or a colon after the salutation, which is *Dear Grandmother*.

Avoid beginning your letter by asking your grandmother how she feels. She wants to know what has happened to you, what you are doing and thinking.

Write at least three paragraphs. Your teacher should help you make corrections before you write a final draft and mail the letter.

1220 Clinton Drive
Eugene, OR 97401
September 15, 0000

Dear Grandmother,

I saw my first bear during our trip to Yellowstone Park this summer. The bear walked in front of our car as we drove into the park. It was black and wasn't as big as I thought it would be.

Last week I wrecked my bike. I was riding down the hill out back of our house and was going too fast to make the turn at the bottom. I skinned my knee, but the front wheel of the bike hit something and is crooked. Dad said he would get it fixed.

I took swimming lessons and liked them a lot. I learned to swim during my third lesson. My sister and I swam nearly every morning at the city pool. We will have to swim now at the YMCA because school is starting.

Love,

Note to Teacher:

You can assign the student to write about some topic other than summer activities. This exercise introduces students to the importance of rewriting. Most students will want such a letter to appear as neat and as perfect as possible.

Some students are unsure when to end a sentence. The optional exercise titled "Basic Statements" that appears at the end of this section should help the student recognize a sentence. You may want to review that lesson before continuing with this study.

My Favorite Dessert

Almost everyone has a favorite dessert. Maybe it's home-made ice cream, the kind that you have to crank in a wooden tub filled with crushed ice. You crank and crank until the handle won't turn. Then the ice cream is ready to eat. Yummy stuff. Or maybe your favorite dessert is chocolate cake or mom's apple pie.

Tell us about your favorite dessert. Describe the dessert. Tell us how it looks, smells and tastes. Write a few sentences and make the dessert so tempting that your readers will want to eat the dessert with you.

Share your description with your teacher. With her help, you can make a few corrections in your report and a second draft will read like frosting on a cake.

Note to Teacher:

If the dessert is something that the student or a member of your family can make, find an excuse to serve it during a meal and invite the student to read the description he/she has written during the meal.

Simple Things: Lesson 5

Spiders

Spiders are the neatest creatures. They climb up the water spout. The rain comes and washes the spiders out. Out comes the sun and dries up all the rain. And you know what happens to the spiders.

So, write your own story about the adventure of a spider. Tell us what the spider looks like, where the spider lives and then what the spider does during this adventure.

When you have completed the story, share it with your teacher. Later, read the story to your family after dinner some night. And send a copy to your grandmother the next time you write to her.

Note to Teacher:

Don't worry about the length of these early stories. Some students will write pages. Other students may be pressed to write a few sentences. The key is to encourage students to write. Look for examples to praise in their reports and stories. Post their work on a family bulletin board or on the refrigerator. Call attention to the writing and other home school projects that the students complete.

If I Could Fly

The dragonfly perches on a rose in the flower garden. It's a busy bug, one with a pencil-like body that zips here and there with the help of two pairs of thin wings. Several dragon-flies have black markings on their nearly transparent wings. Others are a light green, almost chartreuse. Another dragonfly is an amber color but is only half the length as all the rest. What do dragonflies think about? Where do they go when they leave the flower garden?

If you could fly, what would you do? where would you go? Would you jet from shore to shore? from planet to planet? from galaxy to galaxy? In 50 to 100 words explain what you would do if you could fly. You might like to draw a picture to illustrate your report. Share it with your teacher.

Note to Teacher:

With a more advanced writing student, amend the assignment to require the use of action verbs and present tense. You also can increase the maximum number of words to 400 or 500. Another interesting topic is: "I was the last person on earth, and then I heard a knock on the door."

Simple Things: Lesson 7

A Special Place

Your assignment is to write a description of a place that is special to you. That place may be your room, your tree house, the local bakery or zoo. Now visit your special place. Take a sheet of paper and list the following information:

✓ Name and location of your special place
✓ The date of your visit

During your visit, write complete sentences when you record the following information. You may need to write more than one sentence for each answer.

✓ Describe what you *see* during your visit
✓ Describe what you *hear* during your visit
✓ Describe what you *touch* during your visit
✓ Describe what you *smell* and *taste* during your visit

After completing the assignment, share your answers with your teacher. Make certain that you have written complete sentences. As you know, a complete sentence contains a subject and predicate. Underline each subject and circle each predicate so your teacher will know that you know these are complete sentences.

Note to Teacher:

This exercise is the first of two that underscore the importance of using observation and other senses while the student gathers information. This exercise also integrates language study with the development of writing skills.

If your student's favorite place is the local zoo, use this opportunity to incorporate science or some other area of your home school curriculum in a field trip.

Downtown

In your previous assignment, you described what you saw, heard, felt, tasted and smelled in a special place. It's now time to travel downtown and to visit a place that may be foreign to you. Place these questions and write your answers on a clipboard during your 10- to 15-minute stroll through a downtown area or through the business section of a rural community.

You probably will need transportation and someone to accompany you. Ask the person who accompanies you to walk a short way behind so that you can be alone. You will need to concentrate as you write down the following information:

- ✓ Name of the place
- ✓ Location
- ✓ Day and date of observation
- ✓ Describe what you *see* during your visit
- ✓ Describe what you *hear* during your visit
- ✓ Describe what you *touch* during your visit
- ✓ Describe what you *smell* or *taste* during your visit

After you have completed this assignment, write a 100-word report titled "Downtown." Share this report and the information you have collected with your teacher.

Note to Teacher:

It's okay if the student uses such general terms as big buildings, beautiful flowers and smelly smells in describing the downtown area. In the next lesson students will be introduced to similes, which they can use to improve the quality of their writing. Students love to use similes in descriptive writing.

How Big Is BIG?

A simile is a literary device in which one thing is likened to another thing by using the words, *as, as if* or *like*. Examples: He ate *as if* he were famished. A heart *as* big as a whale. "*Like* clouds and wind without rain is a man who boasts of his gifts falsely" (Proverbs 25:14).

Writers use similes to make comparisons that create word pictures in the minds of their readers. Similes are often more effective than writing that something is big. Just how big is BIG, anyway?

Your assignment is to complete each of the following sentences by creating a simile. Then share them with your teacher.

1. He walked as if...
2. The honey was as sweet as...
3. The airplane was as long as...
4. He yelled like...
5. The thunder was as loud as...
6. The cloud looked like...
7. It rained as if...
8. The mountainside climbed like...
9. The pianist played as if...
10. She walked down the street slowly, patiently, like...
11. The wheels on his wagon bumped along the street like...
12. The scream pierced through the quiet night like...
13. The dog's eyes were as hard and unforgiving as...
14. She was as quick as...
15. He hesitated, standing motionless, waiting as if...

Note to Teacher:

Precise detail is another way to report how big something is. For example, the man was 6-foot-10, weighed 285 pounds and wore size 16 shoes. The simile often is a stranger to students, who quickly grow to appreciate this important writing tool.

As an optional assignment, invite the student to share with you any similes he/she discovers while reading during the week. You also can share similes you discover in your reading.

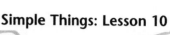

The Butterfly

In our last lesson we learned that a simile is a figure of speech in which one thing is likened to another thing by using the words, *as, as if* or *like*.

In this assignment you are to conduct research on butterflies. Learn all you can about butterflies. Look at pictures. You may discover butterflies on your lawn or in your garden. If so, watch what they do, how they fly. Maybe your family or local library or retail rental outlet has a video about butterflies that you can watch.

Then write a 150-word report in which you describe a butterfly. Include five similes in the report. Underline each simile. Draw a picture of the butterfly using colored pencils or a computer drawing program.

Share your research notes, your written report and the picture you drew with your teacher.

Note to Teacher:

This assignment introduces the student to the importance of research. Encourage the student to consult as many sources as possible, including a local entomologist.

It is time, too, to consider having your student correct errors in the first draft and to complete a second draft of the written assignment.

Don't overlook opportunities to share your student's work with other members of the family.

A Turkey's View

If you were a turkey, how would you view Thanksgiving? That's your writing assignment. Explain how you feel about the holiday and what you might do to celebrate the event.

Have some fun with this assignment. Write a letter to the editor denouncing the holiday and sign it: A. Turkey. Or write an editorial in which you speak out in defense of turkeys. Or write a story in which a turkey deals with Thanksgiving in some novel way.

Write at least 250 words. Also draw a picture of a turkey to illustrate what you have written. Maybe it's a picture of a turkey making tracks, disguising itself as a duck or building a hideout. Share your writing and the picture with your teacher.

Note to Teacher:

You may want to use the first sentence in this lesson to acquaint the student with the subjunctive, indicative and imperative moods as part of your ongoing study of grammar. A plural verb was used in the first sentence of the lesson because the mood is subjunctive, which expressed doubt, a wish or a condition contrary to fact: I wish I were at home. If I were you, I would go. The indicative mood makes a statement or asks questions and calls for singular verbs: He is my friend. Is she a teacher? The imperative mood gives a command: Shut the door.

While the student is assigned to have fun with this lesson, it may challenge a student's assumptions about the holiday. This process is referred to as the development of critical thinking. In this case, Thanksgiving is a national holiday that people enjoy as the beneficiaries of a bountiful harvest, but the holiday might be viewed in an entirely different light if you were a turkey.

The Rabbit Drill

Grammarians tell us that a preposition shows the relation between its object and some other word in the sentence. That definition is helpful if you are a grammarian but not if you are a student or a beginning writer. How do you identify a preposition, and after you figure out what it is, how do you use it?

Rabbits can help. That's right, rabbits. Those critters who can hop around the countryside and nibble on grass and veggies in the garden. They can come to our rescue by performing "The Rabbit Drill." Here's how the drill works. First, you need a tree stump. Place the stump near your house. Second, you need a rabbit. Now, put the rabbit to work.

The rabbit jumps over the stump, under the stump, near the stump, around the stump, beside the stump, and between the stump and the house. The words that tell what the rabbit is doing are called prepositions. Here is a list of words most frequently used as prepositions: aboard, about, above, across, after, against, along, amid, among, around, at, before, behind, below, beneath, beside, between, beyond, by, down, during, except, for, from, in, into, of, off, on, out of, outside, over, round, since, through, throughout, to, unto, under, underneath, up, upon, with, within, without.

Notice, too, that prepositions are followed by a noun, which is called an object when the words are used together as a phrase. If the rabbit jumps over the stump, the phrase is *over the stump.* "Over" is the preposition and "stump" is the object. They make up a phrase or a group of words that contains no verb.

It is important to know how to identify a prepositional phrase because a phrase is not set off by commas. Writers need to know when to use commas. If you know how to run "The Rabbit Drill," you can clear an important hurdle as a writer.[1]

Assignment:

✓ Read three stories that appear in a newspaper. Underline the prepositions and circle all prepositional phrases in each story.

✓ Add prepositional phrases at two or more places in the five basic statements on the next page:

---

1. An optional lesson titled "Clues to Clauses" appears at the end of this section. You may wish to review that lesson before continuing with this study.

1. They ate strawberries.
2. The rain flooded the countryside.
3. The birds will fly south.
4. The telephone rang.
5. He shouted.

✓ Write a 200-word story about a rabbit in which you use 10 or more prepositional phrases. Remember, phrases are not set off by commas.

Feed the Cat

Remember how exciting it is when your family plans to leave home for a holiday outing? What swim suit should I take, what toys will I need, what books do I want to read?

Don't forget, however, about the pets that remain at home. Someone needs to take care of them, which means that someone needs to be told what to do while you are enjoying your vacation.

"Just feed the cat," serves as a satisfactory verbal instruction if the person is acquainted with how you take care of the cat. Often, that type of instruction is incomplete. For example: Does feeding include providing water? What is the cat fed? How much is it fed? When is it fed? Where is it fed? How often is it fed? What about the litter box? What if the cat doesn't show up for a meal? Is the cat to be locked up in a garage at night? Who is to be called if the cat is injured or is missing? Do you have a veterinarian? How can you be reached if an emergency occurs? (If you plan to pay someone for this service, how much money is involved?)

It is a good practice at home or on the job to communicate instructions of this type in writing as well as verbally.

Assignment:

Pretend that you are going on vacation next week. Write instructions for someone who is taking care of your pets. Be precise. Answer the questions listed above and include the days and dates that you plan to be away from home.

Ask your teacher to read your instructions for clarity. If your teacher has questions, rewrite the assignment.

How to Do It

Remember how much fun it is to draw pictures by connecting numbers? The instructions are simple: Draw a line from 1 to 2, etc. until the picture is completed. Painting a picture with oils is more difficult. You need to know what brushes, oils and canvasses to use. You need to know what strokes to make, how to make them, what colors to use.

Words are important in how-to directions. They must be presented in such a way that anyone can follow them to accomplish a task. For example, you may know how to feed the livestock on your ranch, how to build a model airplane, how to check your computer for e-mail messages, how to brush your teeth properly, how to braid your hair, how to mow the lawn, how to drive the family car. Can you explain how to do any of these activities?

Assignment:

Write instructions about how to do something other than feed the family pet. Include a list of equipment and materials that may be needed. Then invite another person to accomplish the task following your written instructions. If the person runs into trouble, find out what created the problem and rewrite that part of your instructions. When you have completed the project, prepare a final draft of your instructions and share it with your teacher.

Note to Teacher:

The person can be anyone but a family member. The student should be present while the person follows the instructions. You may have to help the student find the appropriate words to describe portions of the how-to process.

Remind the student that how-to instructions are important in describing all sorts of activities, including how to assemble a bicycle, to play games and to install computer programs. Technical writing is an important career option, especially in today's rapidly expanding telecommunications field.

Dogs That Talk

"Who says that dogs don't talk?" Jack asked.

Jim replied: "I say so, because dogs aren't people."

"They can talk," Jack said, "because I heard my dog bark at a stray cat."

"That doesn't count," Jim said.

"Does, too."

"No, it doesn't."

The argument continues over whether a dog can talk. Well, maybe dogs don't talk the way people do, but they talk in fairy tales and in make-believe stories. Dog talk can be interesting, especially if it sounds like real talk.

Real talk usually appears inside double quotation marks, which are reserved primarily for this use. Quote marks alert readers that a source's exact words are being recorded. If a dog is speaking, quote marks are also used even though it's make-believe talk or just a common "woof."

Quote marks normally are placed around the full-sentence comment of the person (or dog) speaking. The writer also can use quote marks around single words or phrases that have been spoken. (Your teacher may explain, too, that quotes within quotes are set off by single quote marks.)

It is important to know that the source, or person, who spoke the words is included in the sentence but does not appear inside quote marks. The source may appear in front of, in the middle of or at the end of the quotation as illustrated above in the first three sentences of this lesson. Note that the sources aren't included in the fourth and fifth quotes because by this time the reader knows who is speaking.

Assignment:

Write a 200-word make-believe story in which you report the conversation of two dogs. If you have questions about how to punctuate your direct quotations, ask your teacher.

Example:

Lassie and Shep met at the corral in time to watch the sheep being unloaded from a truck.

"I like working with sheep," said Lassie, a pup who was new to farm life.

"But you're not a sheep dog," responded Shep, the grizzled old timer whose left ear had been chewed off years ago by a bear.

"That doesn't matter," Lassie said, "because I know how sheep think. They will always back off if you look them straight in the eye and crouch near the ground. At least, that's what they say in the books I've read."

Shep tossed his head and with a sheepish look said, "You're just blowing smoke in my face with such fancy talk. You have never seen a sheep in your life."

"Oh, yes, I have," Lassie replied. "I've seen lots of pictures and a video on how to herd sheep. I know I could do it."

"Well, let me tell you that herding sheep ain't easy," Shep said. "I've been herding them for more than 10 years, and they'll surprise you every time. You can't trust them."

Their conversation was interrupted as a section of the corral exploded. Sheep scattered everywhere.

"Go get them," Lassie barked. "You're the sheep dog."

"Sorry," Shep replied. "You chase them. I'm retired."

Note to Teacher:

Remind your student that direct quotations should be broken up with other sentences to avoid repetition, which can bore the reader. Beginning writers, however, often fail to include any direct quotes in a story or article. Direct quotes can add a sense of realism and immediacy.

A Bad Rap

The wolf got a bad rap, according to Jon Scieszka, author of *The True Story of the 3 Little Pigs.* The book, which features the wolf and tells his side of the story, is one of several illustrated books whose authors have rewritten fairy tales and other children's stories.

"Humpty Dumpty Lives"[2] is the title of a story written by Jonathan Nagel, a home school student in Oregon during the winter of 1994. It begins with this paragraph:

> Dr. Smith, a well-known surgeon, was assigned to put the richest egg, Humpty Dumpty, back together. Humpty was on vacation when he accidentally fell from the Eiffel Tower with an awful splat.

The story describes how the doctor used a plastic shell with hinges to unscramble the egg. The story ends:

> This trash-can size egg returned to work as a rich, powerful stockbroker. He decided, however, to face his fears and go back to the Eiffel Tower. When Humpty Dumpty was almost to the top, a gust of wind caused him to fall backward and to bounce down the stairs all the way to the bottom without a scratch.

Assignment:

Use your imagination. Think of a fairy tale or one of your favorite childhood stories and rewrite it. Include several direct quotes in your story and describe the hero or heroine in some detail. Draw a picture to illustrate the hero or heroine of your story.

Note to Teacher:

This writing exercise is a favorite of young writers. They have an opportunity to be creative, which can spark their interest in sharing their thoughts in words and pictures.

In the critique of their work, point out and praise things you like about the story and picture. Writers often enjoy reading their favorite work to other people. In this case, the reading could be to the family after an evening meal.

Simple Things: Lesson 17
Comic Characters

The shortest stories written today appear in newspaper comic sections. Each comic strip of two or more pictures tells a complete story but may be a segment of a continuing story that appears day to day.

Each comic strip has established, well-known characters who appear and act in ways familiar to the reader. These characters do and say things that may be funny but also may be profound, insightful or meaningful. Conversation is critical in communicating the point the cartoonist wishes to make. As you know, the words spoken by these cartoon characters usually appear inside balloons at the top of each picture or panel in the comic strip.

Assignment:

Draw a comic strip that contains three panels. You should have a main character, who is called the protagonist or hero/heroine. As soon as you have a clear picture of the main character, decide what point you want to make in your comic strip. Do you want the main character to say or to do something funny? serious? dumb? insightful? meaningful? Keep the story simple. Only use one other character in the strip. Leave space for balloons that contain conversation at the top of each of the three panels. Draw each panel horizontally on an 8 1/2- by 11-inch sheet of paper. Limit the comments to 10 or fewer words in each balloon. If you were to publish your comic strip in a newspaper, it would be reduced in size.

Note to Teacher:

Even though the student may have no formal art training, this assignment illustrates how character traits may be established visually and how direct quotation often needs to be brief and to the point.

Suggest that the student paste the three panels of the comic strip together. Then find a way to show the strip to members of the family. If several students participate in this project, encourage them to publish a home school comic book.

Don't despair if the student decides to draw pictures of aliens invading the earth or monsters fighting a bloody battle. Remember, you have embarked upon *The Write Stuff Adventure*, one that entails some risk but is tailored to encourage and to equip young people to express themselves in writing, and, in this case, in pictures.

Are Roses Red?

Not all roses are created equal. Some are red. Some aren't. Some have thorns. Others don't. Some emit a fragrance. Others don't. Some grow as trees. Others climb fences and walls. Roses are symbols of beauty and love. They appear at weddings, on Valentine's Day and on other special occasions. Roses are gathered for bouquets on the family dinner table. They also are repugnant to some people, especially those who suffer from hay fever.

In any event, much has been written about roses throughout history, including such rhymes as: Roses are red, violets are blue.

So, let's have some fun with this rhyme and write about roses.

Assignment:

Write a 16-line rhyme that begins with this line: *Roses are red, violets are blue.* Be as silly or as serious as you like, but make certain that your rhyme is in good taste and that the lines rhyme. After your assignment has been critiqued and corrected by the teacher, read your rhyme to members of your family and post it on the refrigerator.

Note to Teacher:

Encourage the student to be positive even though he/she may write a silly rhyme. Explain that good taste means that the writer doesn't make fun of someone in a hurtful manner and that the writer uses language that is acceptable to an audience of strangers.

Journaling Through Life

February 21, 1992—At 11:45 a.m. the room began to roll as though it were made of jelly. An earthquake. My first. Remembering instructions that I received a year earlier after I moved to Southern California, I dove under the oak desk in my university office. I banged against a metal wastebasket and kicked it into the room, thinking that it would be uncomfortable to be stuck under a desk for hours with a wastebasket in my face.

This journal entry may have seemed trivial when it was written, but it documented an important personal experience, one that the writer might wish to review or relive at some later time.

Seminars and workshops are conducted on how to organize and to write entries in a journal. For some people, a journal helps keep track of personal and family history. Writers often keep journals, which may serve as reservoirs for generating story ideas, for developing plots and for creating characters. The key is to establish a time, duration and place for making such entries. As a rule, journals are personal property and are not written to be shared. Otherwise, the writer will be hesitant to pour out his/her heart and soul in a journal.

Assignment:

Write 100 words a day for the next several days in a personal journal. Begin each entry with the date, month and year. Record facts, events and thoughts that occurred during the day.

Note to Teacher:

Because journal writing often is highly personal, the student's work in this lesson should not be shared or critiqued. The lesson may encourage a student to write, however, because thoughts can be expressed in private without worrying about spelling, grammar or syntax. If you find this to be the case, encourage the student to begin journal writing on a consistent schedule.

Basic Statements

A basic statement is a stripped-down, bare-bones sentence. It must, of course, contain a subject and a predicate. Here are five examples of basic statements:

1. The cat slept.
2. What is the forecast?
3. The coach picked Jim.
4. People were hurt.
5. Jill gave a gift.

Notice that each basic statement can stand alone, or it can be expanded. You can add details to the *beginning* and/or the *end* of a basic statement and create a strung-along model. For example:

> During the afternoon *the cat slept* in the dining room of our house in Chicago.

You can add details *inside* the basic statement and create a periodic sentence. For example:

> *The cat*, Tabby, who had been a family pet for 20 years, *slept*.

You also can combine the two models, but the basic statement remains unchanged in each sentence you write. For example:

> During the afternoon *the cat*, Tabby, who had been a family pet for 20 years, *slept* in the dining room of our house in Chicago.

Assignment:

Underline the basic statements in five newspaper articles. Circle the subject and draw a box around the predicate in each sentence.

Copy 10 of the basic statements on a sheet of paper. Make certain that you place a period after sentences that make a statement and a question mark after sentences that ask a question.

Note to Teacher:

This exercise can be used as a review or to acquaint your student with the term, basic statement, which requires a subject and predicate. This exercise also can help the student who writes sentence fragments (i.e., incomplete sentences). If the student cannot identify a subject and predicate, suspend this study of writing until you have reviewed parts of speech, especially nouns and verbs, and such terms as subject, predicate and object. The writing student will be frustrated and unsuccessful without these basic writing tools.

Clues to Clauses

Writers who have trouble with commas failed to learn the basics of grammar. They are unfamiliar with such terms as *phrases* and *clauses* and probably are unable to identify parts of speech. "Basic, Watson," would be Sherlock Holmes' comment if he heard such excuses from anyone confounded by commas.

"Yes," Watson would reply, "but would you give us some clues?"

In this tale, "The Mystery of Clauses," the following clues will solve most of the comma problems that a writer will encounter.

What is a clause?

A clause is a group of related words that contains a subject and a predicate. (Remember that a prepositional phrase contains no verb, only a preposition followed by an object, and a writer does not set off a phrase with commas.)

An independent clause is one that makes sense when it stands alone: *Joe delivered the newspaper*. (This clause is called a sentence. It contains a subject, *Joe*, and a predicate, *delivered*.)

A dependent clause does not make sense when it stands alone: Joe delivered the newspaper *before he left for school*.

(Home schoolers who have learned the parts of speech will recognize that the word *before* is an adverb. When you begin a clause with an adverb, it sounds unfinished, incomplete. Its meaning depends on something else in the sentence. Remove the adverb and the sentence can stand alone as an independent clause.)

Comma Clue No. 1:

All clauses have a subject and a predicate. They're independent unless an extra word has been tacked to the beginning. Look for words like *when, while, during, before, after*. Usually you'll find them hanging out with the adverbs.

Introductory Phrases and Clauses

Use commas to set off long introductory clauses and phrases and some shorter clauses and phrases that would be confusing without the comma.

Examples:

✓ Every day, doctors are asked to perform miracles in hospitals around the world.
✓ To Dean Rea, writing is a familiar word.

Comma Clue No. 2:

When a dependent clause introduces a sentence, set it off with a comma. When a dependent clause follows an independent clause, do not set it off with a comma.

Examples:

✓ Because snow clogged the roads, traffic halted.
✓ Traffic halted because snow clogged the roads.

Comma Clue No. 3:

Grammarians often refer to clauses as being restrictive or non-restrictive, which are confusing terms. Simplify the task by asking the question: Is the clause, phrase or modifier essential to the meaning of a sentence? If it is, don't set it off with commas. Here are some examples:

Essential:

✓ Boys who study will learn. (The clause, *who study*, is necessary to the meaning.)
✓ The bicycle with the bent frame was damaged in an accident. (*With the bent frame* is a phrase and would not be set off by commas. It also is essential to the meaning of the sentence.)

Non-Essential:

✓ Edgar Allen Poe, who wrote "The Raven," is a great American poet. (The clause, *who wrote "The Raven,"* is not necessary to the meaning of the main clause.)
✓ Jane Gray, who sells concert tickets, is a member of our class. (The clause is not necessary. It explains that the girl also sells tickets.)
✓ John Doe, 69, won the award. (Doe's age is called an appositive, which modifies or explains a noun and is never essential to the meaning of a sentence.)
✓ The boy, seeing the clouds, hurried home. (The phrase, *seeing the clouds*, is not necessary.)
✓ Wishing to see the parade, we went to town early. (A participial phrase that begins a sentence is followed by a comma.)

Write a Play

The person who writes a play is called a playwright. This person follows a set format in describing the scenes, the characters, and what they do and say as they appear on the stage.

In this lesson, the assignment is to write a one-act play, which will require the playwright to describe a single scene or stage setting. Only one actor or actress is needed, but two would be ideal. The playwright should plan to act one part. A sister or a brother could act the second part.

The playwright can write a play that is funny or serious. The play should introduce a problem of some sort and should conclude when the problem is solved. For example: A teen-ager encounters difficulty learning to drive.

Format Example:

"John Learns to Drive," a one-act play

The Characters

John . . . . Teen-age boy
Phyllis . . . . John's mother

Scene

Two chairs are the only props on the stage. They are 3 to 4 feet apart and both are facing the audience. John is seated in the left chair facing the audience. Phyllis is seated in the second chair. The scene opens with John holding a make-believe wheel in the driver's seat of a car, his feet resting against make-believe pedals.

JOHN	(shouting) So, what do I do now?
PHYLLIS	(calmly) Release the clutch with your left foot, slowly.
JOHN	(loudly) But I thought that was the brake?
PHYLLIS	No, that is the clutch pedal. The brake is operated by your right foot.
JOHN	Then how do I give it the gas?
PHYLLIS	You mean, how do you depress the accelerator pedal?
JOHN	(in desperation) But the driver's manual says that you start by releasing the clutch and slowly apply the gas.
PHYLLIS	You mean, depress the accelerator pedal.
JOHN	I'm depressed and I haven't even started the car. (pause, don't interrupt laughter)

PHYLLIS	Okay, let's get started. First, make certain the car is in neutral. Then turn the key in the ignition.
JOHN	So, who's got the key? (He takes his hands off the wheel and holds the palms up in a questioning manner.)
PHYLLIS	Have you checked your pockets?
JOHN	(digging into his pockets) Here it is. (He pulls out an imaginary key, holds it up and places it in the ignition just below the steering wheel.)

Assignment:

John obviously has a problem. He works it out as the play continues. The playwright could move the car out of the driveway and have some fun as John careens down the road, desperately turning the wheel, jamming on the accelerator and brake. Mother and son jerk back and forth, stop suddenly. (Include directions on how they are to act and when.) When John gains control of the car, the play ends and everyone lives happily ever after. If John fails, the play is called a tragedy.

Notice that quotation marks do not appear around the words that are spoken by the characters and that directions are enclosed in parentheses.

After the play has been written, recruit any needed characters, rehearse and present the play to members of your family.

Note to Teacher:

This assignment often is a favorite of students. If you are working with a group of home school students, invite them to write the play so that everyone has a part and then stage the play. Or form teams of two to four students and assign each team to write a one-act play. They should also write and print a program. Invite parents and other family members to attend a public performance. Hand everyone a sack of popcorn and enjoy the evening.

The Hero's Journey

Every adventure involves a journey in which people travel to some destination. Cinderella wants to attend the ball but can't because she's poor and mistreated. As the story unfolds, however, Cinderella begins to hurdle increasingly difficult barriers until she succeeds not only in attending the ball, but also in meeting and marrying the prince.

This journey is one that most stories take, and writers learn how to tell what is referred to as "The Hero's Journey." In its simplest story form, a hero is chosen. The hero takes a journey, which is filled with obstacles, including villains. The obstacles become more difficult until the hero conquers them all and reaches the destination. The obstacles may be real or imagined.

Assignment:

✓ Write a 50-word summary of a make-believe story about a hero/heroine who encounters and conquers a villain. List three problems the hero/heroine must solve in reaching a destination. Each problem should be created by the villain and must become increasingly difficult to solve.

✓ Write a 50-word description of the hero/heroine and a 50-word description of the villain.

✓ Write a 1,000-word story told from the viewpoint of the hero or heroine. You cannot be the hero/heroine, which means that you cannot tell the story as though it were your own experience. In other words, do not write a first-person story in which you use such pronouns as I, me and my.

✓ If you wish, draw pictures to illustrate your story.

✓ After the story has been written, critiqued and corrected, complete a final draft and discuss with your teacher ways that the story might be published.

An Example:

The following story illustrates how a writer can tell a story from a heroine's viewpoint:

Jane froze in her tracks as the bull charged around the corner. She eyed the fence and wondered whether she could win another blue ribbon in the 100-meter dash to safety. She was in motion as the question crossed her mind, legs kicking, feet digging into the fresh-plowed soil.

"If only I can make it...," she thought as she stumbled and began a head-long fall just short of the fence.

Note to Teacher:

Before embarking on this project, which may require several weeks to complete, arrange for the student to discuss fiction writing with a free-lance author in your community. A print shop tour will also acquaint the student with how newspapers, magazines and books are published.

If you know of other home school students who are beginning writers, form a study group and invite a writer to teach a short story writing class. The work of the students could be collected and published as a booklet. Copies could be distributed during a student reception attended by parents and friends, which would serve as an incentive and reward for students who are participating in *The Write Stuff Adventure*.

Personal and Family History

Note to Teacher

Reluctant writers often discover that they enjoy researching and recording personal and family history. Maybe it's because they have a vested interest in the subject and it's easy to research. Maybe it's because they have heard the stories told during family meals and gatherings. Whatever the reason, personal and family history can kindle an interest in writing about a subject that is interesting, challenging and rewarding.

The study begins with personal history. Later, the student is introduced to basic interviewing techniques. Mid-way through the study, the scene shifts to experiences of parents, grandparents and other family members, then to a look at the future. When parents are unavailable for interviews, other family members and friends can be substituted.

The study of personal history is not to be mistaken for journaling, which may record impressions, events and descriptions and may not be intended for public viewing. Each assignment serves as an example of how a student can begin creating chapters in a book of history. How those chapters are to be organized into a more complete history is not a subject of this study. Note, however, that a number of organizational choices are available, including chronology and defining moments or crossroads in a person's life.

Establish your expectations as a teacher as you begin this instruction. For example, the student should understand that more than one revision of a writing assignment may be required. The first page of an assignment should contain the author's name and the date the assignment was completed. If a typewriter or computer is used, double space the text and indent paragraphs five spaces. Use an easy-to-read type face rather than an italic, script or bold type face. The students should be encouraged to place a final draft of each assignment in his/her permanent writing file.

Publication should be an objective of this study. For example, a student might select several chapters from this study, design a cover, photocopy the pages, assemble the booklet and share copies with members of the extended family.

Interest in genealogy and in documenting family history continues to grow, especially among retirees. Unfortunately, many valuable resources are no longer living. That fact was borne out when I prepared to write about my maternal grandmother who as a girl had traveled in a covered wagon from Pennsylvania to Kansas. I had heard the story a half century earlier but had failed to record any details in writing. Dates and details had slipped from my mind. The story was lost. Students in *The Write Stuff Adventure* should not encounter this problem if they begin writing and continue to write chapters in their family history.

My Autobiography

As we begin this part of *The Write Stuff Adventure* we need to know something about you, the writer. It's called autobiography, which we will be writing chapter by chapter during this study of personal and family history.

Assignment:

Your first assignment is to write a 200-word summary of your life. Tell it in chronological form, beginning with your birth and continuing until the present time. Report only the highlights. You will be writing personal history in more detail later.

In preparing the first-person report, write your name at the top left side of the first page. Write the date your assignment was completed under your name. Then write the title of your report. Indent each paragraph (five spaces if you are typing or using a computer). Double space your copy. Write on only one side of the paper.

After you have completed your first draft, submit it to your teacher for critiquing. You may be instructed to revise your report several times. Place a copy of your final draft in your permanent writing file.

An Example:

Johnny Doe
Date Report Written

My Life in a Nutshell

I was born under an oak tree at midnight on August 10, 1982, because my dad didn't get mom to the hospital on time. I guess that's why I'm nuts about trees and stuff like that.

When I was about 4, my mom says I used to drag bags of leaves into my room and look at them. I even planted some walnut trees in the garden, but they had to be moved because mom says they were growing in the pea patch.

Then, when I was about 9, I fell out of the big maple tree in the front yard and broke my left arm. I was so interested in looking at all the ants running up and down the tree trunk that I forgot were I was and fell about 20 feet. Luckily, I landed in the hot tub.

I like to learn poems about trees. My favorite is "If Trees Were Only People, I Could Learn to Like Them." I forget the author's name.

When I was 12, I...

Note to Teacher:

This exercise will help the student establish the practice of researching and recording important information such as the date and place of birth. It may be interesting to learn how a student views his/her life in summary form. Don't feel slighted, however, if the child-parent relationship is not included.

Personal and Family History: Lesson 2
First Things First

One of the most fascinating mental games you can play is to search your memory for the first thing you remember about your life. What was it? When did it happen? Where did it occur? What were your feelings? What made the experience memorable? The memory may be a soft, cuddly kitten as a birthday gift. Or it may be a frightening experience. In any event, this early memory is important enough to capture in words as a chapter in your personal and family history.

Assignment:

Write a report about "The First Thing I Remember About My Life." Write your name at the top left side of the first page. Write the date your assignment was completed under your name. Then write the title of your report. Indent each paragraph (five spaces if you are typing or using a computer). Write on only one side of the paper.

An Example:

Dean Rea
Date

The First Thing I Remember About My Life

Lightning lit up the sky and thunder boomed as my parents, my brother and I drove home through blinding rain to our Kansas farm home one summer night in the late 1920s. The storm was one of the first things I remember as a boy and was one of the most frightening things that I have ever experienced.

As the...

Note to Teacher:

Give your student time to think about this assignment. You may, however, have to help the student remember something about his/her early life. Don't hesitate to ask the student to rewrite this assignment after the work is critiqued.

A Memory List

Writers often keep a journal in which they write about events, thoughts and feelings. The list of memories that you complete in this lesson represent journal entries. They will be brief, but they will serve as important reminders of what has been important to you, the author of your personal history.

Assignment:

Read the first word on the list below. Concentrate on the word for a moment before you begin to write. When an image, a remembered smell, sound or color comes to mind, begin writing. Write one or two sentences. Then go to the next word. If a word brings nothing to mind, move on to the next one. Remember that you are writing only about yourself. Write quickly. Write on only one side of a sheet of paper. When you have completed the assignment, share it with your teacher. What you have written in this assignment will be used in Lesson 4.

The Word List:

movie
suitcase
snake
bus
mailbox
sweatshirt
window
snow
bicycle
photograph
library
garden
clock

Note to Teacher:

Invite the student to read his/her responses to you privately and later to the family after an evening meal. Don't critique this written assignment. Encourage the student to concentrate on content rather than on the technical aspects of writing.

Personal and Family History: Lesson 4

I Remember

We learned in Lesson 3 that words can trigger memories. As you read a word in that exercise, pictures flashed across your mind. In each instance, you probably were hard-pressed to limit your summary to a sentence or two. In Lesson 4, you have an opportunity to write in more detail about one of these memories.

Assignment:

Pick one of the personal memories from the list in Lesson 3 and write a 200-word first-person description about that personal memory.

Write your name at the top left side of the first page. Write the date your assignment was completed under your name. Then write the title of your report. Indent each paragraph (five spaces if you are typing or using a computer). Write on only one side of the paper.

Note to Teacher:

Writers use what is called *flashback* when writing about something that occurred in the past. Flashback is defined as a literary device that fills in or supplies background information during the telling of a story. Notice in the following example how something in the present triggers a memory of the past.

An example:

As I waded along an Oregon stream fly fishing in search of the elusive trout, I recalled the day 50 years earlier when I caught my first fish on a lazy creek in Missouri. The day was special for several reasons. I caught my first fish, a perch. Even more memorable was the fact that my father, who was busy harvesting farm crops, took time to teach me how to find the right spot, how to bait a hook and how to wait patiently for the bobber to begin dancing.

The student is not expected to use flashback in Lesson 4. This is a good time, however, to begin introducing students to various literary devices. Later in this study, students will be assigned to work with similes and metaphors.

Require the student to write a second draft after you have critiqued this assignment. Don't forget, however, to point out things you like about a student's work such as action verbs, similes and descriptive words that help paint word pictures in the reader's mind.

Who's Scared?

Most of us enjoy sharing stories about our most frightening experiences while seated around a campfire or during a slumber party. One example might be a story about how a noise in the dark was not made by a grizzly bear but by the family dog, or about your discovery that the shadow that cut across the wall of your bedroom was not that of a burglar but of your brother.

I recall a night walk along a rural road. It was a shortcut I took after playing a seventh grade basketball game. Moonlight illuminated the road that ran near farm fields and eventually through a grove of oak trees near my home. My thoughts of the ball game quickly switched to thoughts of ghosts and goblins as I walked the half mile home. A log bridge spanned a creek at the fringe of the oak grove. And I began to wonder about the headless horseman I had read about. Could I make it across the bridge? Would I escape through the oak grove? Even though I was hobbling on a sprained ankle, I made a dash for it, only to be confronted midway through the oak grove by a man in the dark. Oh, no, the headless horseman? My heart stopped. Then I heard my father say, "Hello, son. I didn't want you to walk alone in the dark."

Assignment:

Write a 200- to 300-word story about one of your most frightening experiences. If possible, maintain the suspense until the end of the story. Describe your thoughts and reactions as well as the event.

Write your name at the top left side of the first page. Write the date your assignment was completed under your name. Then write the title of your report. Indent each paragraph (five spaces if you are typing or using a computer). Double space and write on only one side of the paper.

Note to Teacher:

This is a popular exercise among students. After it is written and corrected, invite the student to read the story to members of the family. That sharing opportunity is another form of publication, which is encouraged as part of *The Write Stuff Adventure.*

Personal and Family History: Lesson 6

Here and Now

While writing our personal and family history, we may think so much in the past that we lose sight of the present. Today's details and thoughts are quickly lost as we cope with busy schedules. What may be important to us today may become only a hazy outline in the future. Therefore, those events and thoughts that are important to us should be captured as they occur, which is a reason that keeping a journal is important for a writer.

Assignment:

Write a 200- to 500-word report titled "Here and Now" in which you look up from your notebook, typewriter or computer and describe the place where you are working and the thoughts that cross your mind.

An Example:

From a clock to my left a blue bird with beady black eyes pops out of a little door. "Cuckoo! Cuckoo! Cuckoo!" it sings, then springs back inside, the door closing behind it. "Cuckoo! Cuckoo! Cuckoo!" Little birds burst out of their doors like popcorn exploding in a hot pan.[2]

Note to Teacher:

Note that the student has used action verbs and has written in the present tense, which creates a sense of immediacy.

This exercise is not intended to test a student's ability to organize thoughts, only to express them in writing. The description should be as precise as possible.

---

2. Written by Holly Reinhard, a home school student.

My Favorite Pet

You may have a pet, probably a dog or a cat, and enjoy telling other people about your pet. In describing your pet you may use such terms as big, little, fluffy, long, short and heavy. If you want to emphasize a description, you probably use the word, "very."

These are perfectly good words but often they are not as descriptive as you might like. For example: How big is big? How big is very big? To an ant, a grasshopper may be big and a horse may be very big.

Writers use similes to make these comparisons. Students are delighted to make friends with this literary device. The simile is easy to identify and easy to use. Examples: My dog looks *like* a mop. My cat's tail is *as* big as an elephant's trunk. He ate *as if* he were starved. Note the italicized words, *like, as, as if*. They are used to make these comparisons.

Here are examples of how different students have described their favorite pets:

✓ His whiskers sagged *as if* they were made of string.
✓ His feet make a pedaling motion *as if* he is riding an imaginary bicycle.
✓ He has eyes that look like *chocolate* drops.
✓ Having a puppy in the house is *like* having a newborn baby.
✓ When you play catch and throw the ball to her, she is off *like* a missile homing in on its target.
✓ He could pull *like* a tow truck.

Assignment:

Write a 250-word story about your favorite pet. Include the pet's name, how old you were when you received the pet, your pet's physical description and things your pet does during the day. If you have never had a pet, write about one of your favorite toys. Be sure to include similes in your descriptions.

Note to Teacher:

Study the examples above and note that the similes are not set off by commas.

When similes are overused, they become cliches. Examples: Clean as a whistle. White as snow. Don't worry, however, if the beginning writer uses a cliché which he/she may have picked up while reading.

The metaphor is a related literary device with which a writer should be acquainted. The metaphor is likening one thing to another without the use of the words *like* or *as*. The comparison is implied, making the image more vivid than it might be in a simile. Examples: His singing was sweet honey to their ears (metaphor); His singing was *like* sweet honey to their ears (simile).

The Day I Was Born

Thus far in this study, the assignments have drawn material based primarily on the writer's experiences. The help of other family members becomes important in the following lessons. Therefore, the art of asking questions is one that will be developed during *The Write Stuff Adventure.*

In formal interviewing, the person asking the questions is called the interviewer, the person answering the questions is called the respondent. In this study, you are the interviewer and must think through the questions that are to be asked of the respondent before the interview takes place.

In preparing questions, you should ask: What is the purpose of the interview? What do I want to find out? As soon as the focus of the interview has been determined, you can write a list of several questions you expect to ask during the interview.

There are several types of interview questions. The most popular invite "yes" or "no" responses. Example: "Is it true that you were you born on April 18, 1929?" This type of question is fine if the interviewer is confirming the spelling of names, facts and figures. The "open-ended" question is more useful in most interviews. For example, rather than ask the respondent if he/she ever owned a car, ask something like this: "Tell me about the first car you owned." The respondent's answer will suggest additional questions about the subject.

Arrange a time and place to conduct an interview. Make certain that you explain the purpose and focus of the interview. A personal face-to-face interview is preferred, and arrange to be alone with the respondent so that other people don't interrupt. Take notes. Write on only one side of a sheet of paper and don't hesitate to ask the respondent to repeat a statement, especially one that you may want to use as a direct quotation.

Assignment:

Talk to one or to both of your parents about the day you were born. Find out all you can about the day. For example: When and where were you born? What was the weather like? Were you born in a hospital? Were you late in arriving? Were your parents excited? Was there anything unusual about your birth or about the day you were born? Make certain that the exact time and place of birth is recorded, and include your birth length and weight.

Take written notes while you are conducting an interview and turn them in with a 300-word report titled "The Day I Was Born." Use as few personal pronouns as possible.

Note to Teacher:

1. The student should establish a focus, which obviously is to learn as much as possible about his/her birth. In some cases this may be impossible because of the unavailability of parents and others acquainted with the birth. An alternate assignment might be for an adopted child to find about how his/her new parents felt the day he/she arrived.

2. The student should write a half dozen questions to ask at least one respondent, which could be the mother or father. These questions may change from person to person. Review these questions with the student before the interview in a role-playing situation.

3. The student should be prepared to stray from the list of written questions during the interview. The beginner frequently fails to follow up on a response. For example, in talking with his/her mother the student may learn that the birth didn't take place in a hospital or in a home but in a car. Of course, that response raises all kinds of questions that should be asked before the student proceeds to the next written question on his/her list.

Students love this assignment. It is non-threatening because most of them know something about their birth. Filling in the details about how mom and dad felt and responded to the birth is important and should be recorded.

Unless the student has interviewing experience, one respondent will be adequate for the assignment. If both parents are interviewed, they should be interviewed separately.

Dad's Car

My dad's favorite car was a light brown SAAB. He bought it new in 1973 for $4,000. It had four doors, a four-speed transmission and got 20 miles to the gallon. It was the first car he had owned that had front-wheel drive, which gave it good traction. The car rode smoothly and silently.[3]

The student went on to report that while the SAAB had numerous safety features, repairs often required up to two weeks because parts were not readily available. Eventually, the car was sold for $1,000 because "it got too expensive to keep."

This chapter in the student's personal and family history only required a short interview with his father and less than a half hour of writing time. The student's mother critiqued the draft and a final draft was written.

Granted, this type of information may appear to be inconsequential to most readers, but it records details about people, places and things that are important to future generations. For example, it is interesting to review the family ledger and to learn the prices paid for houses, vehicles and other appliances during the past half century. The cost of a house purchased in the 1950s may be sufficient for only a down payment on a house today.

Assignment:

Interview your father or some other adult member of your family about which one of the cars he has owned was his favorite and why. Then write a 200-word report. Include at least two sentences that are direct quotes spoken by the respondent. The focus of your report is to explain why this was the favorite car. Seek details about the make, model, price, color and mechanical features of the car and when it was purchased. Explain why the car was purchased and how it was used. How old was the respondent at the time? How much did gasoline cost per gallon when he purchased it?

Note to Teachers

As is true of many of these assignments, the student should strive to gather anecdotes that help tell the larger story. This also offers the student an opportunity to use similes and to be precise in describing a person, place or thing. The problem often occurs when the student

---

3. Written by Brook Reinhard, a home school student.

fails to follow up with questions during an interview in which more specific descriptions and information may be needed when the assignment is written.

Remind the student that direct quotation should appear inside double quotes and that the source normally is set off by a comma. Example:

"I drove that rattle-trap of a car until one wheel fell off," he said. "I don't know what happened to the car, but I think dad sold it as junk after it quit running in 1944."

Remember that rewriting is important. Sometimes a second and third draft may be required before the student is prepared to place the assignment in a permanent writing file.

Something Special

Children love to hear stories about the good old days, especially about important events in the lives of their parents. Often children have heard stories shared by parents at mealtime. Some of these stories are humorous. Others may be more serious and may reflect important milestones in a person's life. In any event, these stories often are shared repeatedly during family gatherings as the years pass.

While such oral history serves a good purpose, much of it should be recorded and preserved in a written family history. It's great during annual Thanksgiving dinners for Aunt Maime to retell the story of how she outran and outfoxed a bull that chased her across a field on the family farm 40 years ago. Next time she tells the story, take notes and write the story as soon as the dishes are dried.

Assignment:

Interview your mother or some other adult female member of your family about something special that occurred during her childhood. Maybe she will share some humorous event with you. Include the time and the place.

Write a 300-word report. Include at least two sentences of direct quotation.

And the next time Aunt Maime or some other member of your family tells an interesting story, write it down and add it to your personal and family history.

Personal and Family History: Lesson 11

School Daze

Home schooling wasn't an option when I was a boy. You packed a lunch, climbed on a bus and spent as much as an hour traveling to school. The older kids were certainly undemocratic about deciding where everyone sat on the bus. The bullies on the playground also made life difficult for those of us who weren't fighters. You used all of your people skills just to stay out of trouble.

One school experience stands out in my mind, however. It occurred during fourth grade. For several weeks, playing marbles was a craze during morning recess. All of the boys brought marbles, dropped one in the center, and drew straws to determine the order of shooting. Great fun, I found, until I learned that if a person shot a marble out of the ring, he got to keep it. That meant some people were losers. A game that I had played for fun turned out to be a game of "keepers" and "losers," which somehow didn't square with my sense of healthy competition. So, I quit after the first game, losing a marble and a sense of innocence.

That story is one I might share if a son or daughter were to interview me. I could tell it slowly and in such a way that they could take adequate notes. I would attempt to offer the insight about my disappointment with what I thought was a perfectly innocent game, a matching of skills and not a matter of "keeping" the spoils.

Assignment:

Interview your mother or your father about what he/she remembers most about attending grade school. Each parent will have a different story to tell. Maybe it was the school building itself. Maybe it was the sack lunches students brought to school and often traded. Maybe it was a game students played during recess. Maybe it was a friend. Maybe it was a bully. Maybe it was a teacher. Maybe it was several things that made school special.

Your report should be 200- to 300 words in length and should be doubled spaced if you are using a typewriter or a computer. Include at least two direct quotations from your respondent. Avoid using personal pronouns.

Example of a story's introduction:

> Audrey Franks enjoyed watching the wind create various patterns in the wheat fields that surrounded her two-mile walk to school each morning as a first-grader.

"I never thought about being lonesome even though I walked to school alone," Audrey said. "I had the wind to keep me company. Oh, how the wind blew on those Kansas prairies."

Note to Teacher:

Students probably will find it difficult to switch from writing about "my mother" or "my father" to using their names. While the use of personal pronouns is acceptable in writing personal and family history, the student should become familiar with reporting what he/she is told, sees, hears and smells. This is referred to as the objective report, one in which the writer removes himself/herself from the story.

This form of writing also underscores the importance of including detailed information in any personal or family history account: Who and how old was the person? When and where did the event occur?

Personal and Family History: Lesson 12

Family Heirloom

One of the many old things my family and I enjoy is a Philco radio-record player. It is about 70 years old. My grandpa gave it to us as a house-warming present when we moved into our new log house. He bought it from one of his friends.

The cabinet is laminated wood with tiny inlaid wood stripes. It is about 3 feet tall, 3 feet wide and a little over 1 foot deep. When we tilt out the front panel, we can see the turntable sitting on the speaker. It has really good sound.[4]

The student goes on to describe in some detail the 78 rpm records from the 1930s that came with the radio-record player. In this case, the student has used first person, which adds a personal touch to the story. The reader is offered a time frame through reference to the 1930s, and the student has included the date the story was written at the top of the manuscript.

Your family, too, has an object that holds special meaning. It may be an heirloom, an antique, something that is displayed, shared or referred to at family gatherings. These things help create a sense of family, a thread that binds generation to generation. They are an important part of your family history.

Assignment:

Write a 300- to 400-word report about an antique or object that is important to you and to your family. It may be a clock that was owned by your great-great-grandparents, or a violin that an ancestor played while performing on Broadway. It may be a book, a candlestick, a picture.

You should, of course, describe the object and explain why it is important to the family. You may have to talk to several members of the family to collect the information you need.

Your description should be as precise as possible. How big is a big clock? How beautiful is a flower? How wide is the ocean? How high is the sky? Use similes for comparisons.

Continue placing the date the story is written at the top of the page along with your name. Double space the manuscript.

---

4. Written by Daniel Nott, a home school student.

Note to Teacher:

It is important that the student continue the practice of placing the date the manuscript was written and his/her name at the top of the first page. This practice should become routine with all written communication, including notes and instructions.

Not all students are successful in correcting all errors in a second draft. As we move along in *The Write Stuff Adventure* it may become necessary for a student to revise a second, even a third time. This process is called "polishing" an article and is a standard practice for many professional writers as well as for students.

Also note that the student is assigned to turn in notes with the first draft. Incomplete notes often make it difficult to write a satisfactory story. If you find noun-less and verb-less half-phrases, suggest the student practice writing full-sentence notes. Maybe the student needs to slow the pace when conducting an interview, thus providing time to write adequate notes.

As an incentive, remind your student of plans to make copies of this personal and family history available to other members of the extended family. Suggestions appear in the Project lesson.

Personal and Family History: Lesson 13

Valentine's Day

Ever wonder how your grandparents met? about their courtship? about the first few years of their marriage? These are stories that are sometimes shared at family reunions and at wedding anniversaries. Normally, they were happy times, special times that grandparents may be willing to share with you.

For example, a student discovered that her grandmother was 16 years old when she danced with a 17-year-old boy at a school dance. "It was love at first sight," the grandmother admitted. They were married five years later and reared a family of 10 children. They were still dancing at their golden wedding celebration.

Assignment:

Interview your grandparents and find out how they met and something about their courtship. If only one grandparent is available, talk to that person and base your report on that interview.

Your report should be 300- to 400 words in length and should include at least two direct quotations.

Include some biographical information about each grandparent, the date and place they met and the date of their marriage. Attach your notes to the back of the report you submit to your teacher.

Note to Teacher:

It may be impossible for students to interview grandparents in person. In such a case, arrange for the student to contact grandparents by telephone. In some cases, the student may have to write a letter or to send an e-mail message containing the questions. If a reply fails to supply all of the needed information, encourage the student to follow up with additional questions.

A Family Yarn

One of the most interesting stories written by a student of mine was in response to the "family yarn" assignment in this lesson. Students were instructed to interview a grandparent about something unusual that occurred during childhood. Here's the result:

The Sticky Firecracker

When my grandpa starts telling stories about when he was young, they usually are about him getting in trouble. In one story that he told me he didn't get caught.

My grandpa's dad owned a Nash garage. One of his dad's friends was a mechanic who worked there. One day the mechanic wasn't doing anything and told my grandpa that he knew how to make firecrackers. He sent my grandpa, who was 12, to the drug store to buy some potassium.

When the pharmacist asked my grandpa what he was going to do with it, he said a friend of his dad's was going to show him how to make firecrackers. The pharmacist told him to be careful as my grandpa ran out the door.

When he got back to the shop, the mechanic mixed the potassium with some sulfur until it was a paste-like substance. Then he rolled it out flat. Next he took a piece of conduit, a metal tube, and sharpened it so it was like a cookie cutter. He cut the dough into circles about the size of a nickel and laid them out to dry. The mechanic told my grandpa that when they dried he could hit them with a hammer and they would make a loud bang.

Out behind the Nash garage was a track that the logging train followed. My grandpa heard the train coming, grabbed a firecracker and ran outside. The firecracker had dried about an hour but it was still a little sticky. He set it on a track and ran back into the garage. He looked out the window and saw the train wheel hit the firecracker. The next second he heard a bang as loud as a gun.

The engineer stopped the train and jumped out. He started squirting oil on the wheel. Then he got back in the train and it started moving slowly. Because the firecracker was still a little moist, it stuck to the wheel. As the wheel turned, the firecracker made another bang. The engineer jumped out again, looked under the train and on the wheel but didn't see anything.

So, he got in the train and it started again. My grandpa came out and watched the train drive off making a bang every time the wheel went around.

Later, my grandpa said he put the rest of the firecrackers on an anvil and hit them with a hammer. "They nearly blew the hammer out of my hand," my grandpa recalls.[5]

Assignment:

Interview a grandparent, a great-grandparent or some other elderly member of your extended family. Find out something unusual that happened to that person while he or she was a child. Maybe it was the time your grandfather went hunting for rabbits with a sling-shot as a boy and stumbled onto a bear. Maybe it was the time your grandmother spilled a pie she had baked while serving her teen-age friends. The incident or event should be unusual and interesting, and it should be one that stands out in the mind of your grandparent.

Your report should be at least 400 words in length. Attach your notes to the back of the report you submit to your teacher.

Note to Teacher:

While I enjoy reading "The Sticky Firecracker" story, it could be improved by rewriting and using more direct quotation. This is an example of how a writer often does the telling rather than letting the source do it. It is the reason why a beginner should strive to include direct quotes periodically in a story of this type.

---

5. Written by Daniel Nott, a home school student.

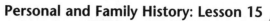
A Family Photo Album

Family albums are filled with photographs of ancestors whose names have been forgotten. No one took time to write captions that identified the people by name or documented the time and place where the photograph was taken.

"Oh, I'll remember that," is the rationale that runs through the mind of a person who slips a photograph into an album. The problem, of course, is that this information is unavailable to future generations. So, get in the habit of writing a captions to identify each photograph in an album. Also date and file negatives.

Assignment:

✓ Select a photograph in your family album, identify the people in the photograph and write a 100-word report that completes the story. What were the people doing? Where were they? What was the date?

✓ Write captions for five other photographs in the album. Each cutline should identify the people, the place, the event and the time.

Personal and Family History: Lesson 16

Oral History

Oral history is important for several reasons. The storyteller relates the story in a personal way, using inflections and idioms that are unique to an individual and to a culture. It is important to document experiences and to identify people from generation to generation. It also is important to preserve a sense of realism, a feeling of personal identity. Preserving these stories on a tape recorder and on film are ways to accomplish this goal.

Sometimes a son or a daughter can remind a parent or grandparent of favorite stories while such recording sessions are conducted. For those people who do not have time to write the stories, the tape recorder and video serve as a library that can be consulted later.

Assignment:

Interview a grandparent or an elderly member of your extended family using a tape recorder or a camcorder that records sound and images. Encourage your grandparent to share a story with you, preferably one that you have heard him or her tell before. You may need to ask questions during the interview.

Make certain that the tape recorder is operating properly. The cassette also should be used only for the interview and should be preserved as part of the family's oral history.

After you have completed the assignment, arrange to share the recording or the video with members of the family. Then place the cassette in your family library.

You also should write a note in which you describe the interview, including the person you interviewed, the date and the place. The notes should then be placed in your permanent writing file.

Note to Teacher:

This assignment is popular with students. If your family doesn't own a tape recorder, borrow one. More likely, you will have access to a camcorder.

Encourage the student to begin the session by recording the following information: The student's name, person being interviewed, date, place and interview topic.

Example: This is John Doe interviewing my grandmother, Agness Nash, on March 8, 1998, in Buffalo, N.Y., about the time she rode across the United States in a train in 1902.

Things with Wings

Remember your first airplane ride? White knuckles? Thoughts of dying on takeoff? The snacks served aboard the airliner? The baby who sat in the next seat and screamed during the two-hour trip? The relief of landing safely?

Remember the airplane? For some people it might have been a bi-wing, fabric-covered, open-cockpit Jenny of World War I vintage. For others, it might have been a Boeing 707. Eventually, it may be an intergalactic spaceship. In any event, a first airplane ride is often a memorable one.

Assignment:

Write a story about someone's first airplane ride. It can be your own. Or perhaps a great-grandparent may have a story of a pioneer flight, something like that of Ezra Meeker, who traveled The Oregon Trail by ox cart in 1852, by automobile in 1916 and in an airplane in 1924.

Describe the airplane and how the passenger felt before, during and after the flight. What happened during the flight? What made it memorable other than the fact that it was the first flight?

Maybe you have a family member who is or has been a pilot. You may decide to interview that person about his/her experiences. Decide on an interview focus before arranging to discuss the subject with your source.

If you interview someone, include at least two direct quotations in the report. Attach your interview notes to the back of the report you submit to your teacher.

A Bedtime Story

My favorite bedtime story is not one but numerous stories that I told my brother when we were youngsters living on a 40-acre farm in southern Missouri. We slept in the same bedroom, and each night he would tune in a mythical radio station we called KMNO. While I fabricated the next installment of "Pete, the Cat" in my mind, I would stall by instructing my brother he wasn't tuned in yet to the right station.

I have forgotten the individual stories, except that they were adventure yarns, but I vividly recall the setting and the era in which they were told. Except for an occasional recounting around a dinner table at family reunions, this happening in life has not been documented in any detail. I wonder if it was instrumental in my choosing writing as a career.

Assignment:

Write a 200- to 500-word report in which you identify your favorite bedtime story, how old you were when you read or were told the story and why the story is your favorite.

A Ten-Year Plan

"What do you plan to be doing in 10 years?"

"Hey, I don't know what I'm gonna be doing tomorrow, and you wanna know what I'll be doing in 10 years?"

"You should have a plan, some goal."

"But it might change."

"Certainly, but you can amend it."

"I haven't really thought about what I'll be doing in 10 years."

"Sure, you have in general terms. Your thoughts about the future will begin to crystallize as you express them in written form."

Assignment:

Write a 500-word report describing what you would like to be doing in 10 years and why.

Personal and Family History: Project

A Family History

This project is a frosting-on-the-cake assignment that you have been looking forward to for months. It's time to publish the chapters you have written in this never-ending book of thoughts, stories and memories.

Review the stories you have written in this study and select those you wish to share with members of your extended family. You may find that one or two are rather personal and should remain that way.

If you have used a computer to write your stories, increase the type size of your headlines and single space the text.

Write a headline and a block of copy for a cover page that can be printed on heavier paper. The headline can be: "A Personal and Family History" or something more creative. The copy block should explain who wrote the stories, your age and something about the study. A brief family history also could be incorporated. Pick a colorful paper for the front and back covers to the booklet, but print the stories on white paper, so they will be easier to read.

Prepare enough copies of your booklet for distribution to members of the extended family.

For those of you who plan to add chapters to your personal and family history, reserve a computer floppy disk for this purpose and place a printed copy of your history in a loose-leaf notebook.

Show and Tell

Writers are often encouraged to "show" rather than to "tell," which may be a difficult distinction for beginners.

Briefly stated, the writer "tells" a story from a personal point of view, which requires the use of first-person pronouns. Examples: *my* father, *our* family, *I* shouted.

To "show" the writer must step outside the story and write it from the viewpoint of an impersonal observer. First-person pronouns are omitted. Following the examples above, *my father* is referred to by name, George Rea. *Our family* is referred to as the Rea family, and *I shouted* would be written: Dean Rea shouted.

Even though the first person is often the viewpoint taken by a writer of personal and family history, now is a good time to practice "showing" your readers what occurred.

Assignment: Tell

First, make mental notes during your next meal. Then in a 200-word first-person report *tell* what you ate and did during the meal, what you smelled, heard and saw.

Example: My mouth watered as my mother set a steaming bowl of white potatoes, a platter of thick steaks and a basket of biscuits in the middle of the table.

Assignment: Show

Then in a 200-word report *show* what took place during the meal by describing the food, the diners, the smells, the sounds, the words spoken and happenings without using first-person pronouns.

Example: A steaming bowl of white potatoes joined a platter of thick steaks and a basket of biscuits in the center of the table as the family sat down for dinner.

Note to Teacher:

This assignment can be difficult for the student who is accustomed to writing in first person. It may be helpful to point out that the writer is more of an impersonal reporter than an active participant in the "show" example above. The deletion of first-person pronouns is further illustrated in the next lesson.

This exercise also will help prepare the student for the units dealing with the essay and with non-fiction article writing.

Personal and Family History: Optional

This I Believe

It is important in writing personal and family history to record views and beliefs. For example: If your grandfather is a staunch supporter of a political party, you might interview him and find out why.

Most people hold strong views about certain topics. These beliefs are expressed in the first person, e.g., "I believe that..." While such an approach is common, the writer can express the same view without using personal pronouns. In the following examples, remove the personal references and restate the point of view:

✓ I believe that a good way to handle this matter is by a vote. (A good way to handle this matter is by a vote.) (This issue could be settled by voting.)
✓ You can't help liking this book. (This book is captivating.)
✓ In my opinion smoking causes cancer. (Smoking causes cancer.)

The writer can marshal arguments to support each of these viewpoints in composing a point-of-view essay or editorial expression.

Assignment:

Write a 250-word report on a topic about which you feel strongly. Do not, however, use personal pronouns. You could, for example, write about patriotism, or the importance of the family in today's society, or the benefits of home schooling.

Note to Teacher:

Public speaking is a dying art. Despite the popularity of verbal expression, many people are terrified when invited to appear before an audience. They spend valuable time excusing their stage fright, saying such things as: "I've never done this before and I'm so nervous." Such statements embarrass the audience as well as the speaker.

This lesson offers one of many opportunities during *The Write Stuff Adventure* for a student to write and deliver a speech. For example, after the report is polished, invite the student to read it to members of the family. Encourage the student to stand while reading the report, to make eye contact with members of the audience and to speak loudly and slowly enough to be heard. Other principles of public speaking can be introduced as you feel they are appropriate.

The topic of patriotism mentioned earlier in this lesson suggests another opportunity to encourage and to challenge your student. Service organizations like the American Legion often sponsor writing and public speaking contests. Take note of such contests and encourage the student to enter them.

Section Three:

The Essay Made Easy

Note to Teacher

After teaching for more than three decades, I am convinced that anyone interested in pursuing the writing craft should learn how to organize and to write an essay before tackling other forms of non-fiction and fiction. That instruction should occur as soon as the student has acquired basic language and writing skills and has some experience in gathering information.

The essay teaches and helps sharpen a number of skills, including information-gathering, critical thinking and organizing. The essay form, however, often is criticized by beginners because of its rather rigid structure.

"I want to be a creative writer" is the excuse some students offer, which is another way of saying they want to work without boundaries and organizational constraints. Unless they are experienced writers, their "creative" work often turns out to be no more than rambling thoughts. If students study fiction and non-fiction, they will learn that the organization of most written expression follows basic formats. I was surprised, for example, to learn that the "The Hero's Journey" (page 45) forms the basic organizational model for the short story and novel. The writer introduces a problem and the hero strives against increasing odds to solve the problem. What appears to be "creative" writing follows a rather rigid format.

The basic learning tool is the five-paragraph essay, which a student can use to write such things as a report, a term paper, a research document, an editorial, a speech or a non-fiction article. The essay also teaches the writer to focus on one central issue or point, a skill that is critical in such other forms of writing as the non-fiction article, the non-fiction news report, the short story and the novel.

The first question, and the most critical, that a writer or a public speaker asks should be: What is the point of the story or of the speech? More written and spoken communications fail to inform or to persuade an audience for this reason more than any other.

"I can't write the lead" is a common complaint heard in newsrooms and in journalism school writing labs. "I can't get started. I must have writer's block," say seasoned reporters and students alike.

In most cases, the writer simply hasn't identified the essential point of the story. Of course, this is oversimplification of an often complex problem, but writing the introduction of any manuscript is impossible without knowing what the focus is to be, and that decision is the writer's responsibility. Helping the writer recognize and refine that focus often is the role of an editor or a teacher.

Here's how the process can work with beginners in essay writing:

The focus or point of the essay is often referred to as the thesis statement. Students should be encouraged to limit that statement to a single sentence of 25 words or less.

"No problem," the student says. "I want to write about home schooling."

"Sorry, that won't work. Be more specific."

"Well, I like home schooling."

"How strongly do you feel about home schooling?"

"Well, I believe everyone should be home schooled."

"Great! You have a point of view that can be argued."

The point of view appears as the thesis statement at the end of the first paragraph in a five-paragraph essay. Three supporting arguments follow and the thesis statement is restated in the fifth paragraph. If concessions or additional arguments are appropriate, the number of paragraphs may be increased.

While the traditional form may be a point-of-view essay, it can be used to write an informational report, a term paper or a research document. For example, a student may be assigned to write a report about some subject that he/she is studying in history, literature or science. While the report may not express a personal view, a teacher can help make the writing assignment interesting and can help encourage critical thinking if the focus of the report is more specific and expresses a point of view.

"Write a 10-page report on the Civil War" is an invitation for a student to regurgitate the textbook or some other informational source. That type of assignment often serves a purpose, but a questionable one, if the objective is to encourage students to learn how to write. Report writing can be used, for example, to determine whether the student has read the material.

Unfortunately, the student isn't challenged to think. Pick a few phrases and sentences, copy them and turn in the report. That behavior might change if the student were assigned to write about the most interesting or significant Civil War battle, which requires a bit of reading, a bit of analysis, a bit of critical thinking. The battle becomes the focus of the report, which should include the reasons why the student considers a particular battle more important than the others. Note, too, that the student has been involved in the process by determining which battle is the most significant. Now the student has something at stake in the project and should be motivated to prove that point in the written assignment.

A student could then be encouraged to write a separate fictionalized report describing the battlefield, the battle and what the soldiers say and think. A high school student, for example, might compare the life of soldiers in the Civil War with those in the classic novel, *All Quiet on the Western Front*. The possibilities are endless. Writing, as a result, becomes a useful tool of expression, a real adventure in communicating information, thoughts and ideas.

Extensive teacher involvement may be needed to help beginners identify and write a suitable thesis statement. That involvement should shift, however, to an after-the-fact critique as a student matures as a writer.

As you will see later in our study, the essay form provides a means for making concessions to other points of view and/or to conflicting facts and information. This is important in developing a student's critical thinking and in helping a student realize the importance of becoming acquainted with as many sides of an issue as possible. The result should lead to reasoned argumentation and persuasion rather than to the expression of dogmatic statements of opinion.

As you begin this study, review your expectations as a teacher. For example, the student's name and the date the assignment was completed should appear at the top of the first page. Typed copy should be double spaced and paragraphs should be indented five spaces. Remind the student that more than one revision may be required. A final draft of each assignment should be placed in the student's permanent writing file.

The Thesis Statement

In writing an essay, the initial task is to establish a focus. In other words, what is the point that you are trying to make?

In this lesson, you will be asked to write separate sentences of 25 words or less in which you express a personal opinion. Typically a student will respond with something like the following sentences:

- ✓ No. 1: Do all dogs go to heaven?

- ✓ No. 2: The average American watches more than seven hours of television every day.

- ✓ No. 3: I believe everyone should be home schooled.

No. 1 fails to express a point of view.

If No. 2 were factually correct, it would be inappropriate as a thesis statement because it fails to express a point of view.

No. 3 is the student's statement that appeared in the overview section of this chapter. It is not an ideal topic because it is too broadly stated. As a home school teacher, however, I would work with it for several reasons. Initially, it is more important for the student to learn how to organize an essay than to be overly concerned about the content. The student is acquainted with the subject and little research would be required. It also originated with the student, which can be used to motivate the student to continue through the process.

Assignment:

Submit three sentences of 25 words or less. Each sentence should contain an argument or a point of view about some topic or issue. Base each argument on a subject you are studying or on some issue that your family has discussed during a meal. In a later assignment you will be required to offer information that will support or defend your arguments. Therefore, it is important that you select arguments that you can defend rather than simple statements of opinion.

Refining the Thesis

Before you proceed with organizing and writing the essay, the subject should be further researched. The writer who begins a manuscript without information is ill prepared to convince an audience that the message is worth the effort of reading, let alone persuasive enough to change a reader's viewpoint.

Information and focus walk hand-in-hand. So, the hours you invest in learning how to conduct research in a library, on the Internet or through personal interviews is as foundational to writing as are the skills developed through the study of language, grammar, punctuation and spelling.

In the interest of moving through this first point-of-view essay, let's work with a topic that can be discussed without researching it and base the essay on a student's experience with home schooling. In an earlier lesson the following thesis statement was suggested:

I believe that everyone should be home schooled.

Our first step is to convert the first-person statement to a non-person statement, which is easy to accomplish. Some teachers may argue that a point-of-view essay should be written from a first-person (I, me, my) viewpoint. I would agree if the teacher later assigns the student to remove first-person references to illustrate 1) how wordy such essays can be and 2) how points of view can be expressed without personal references.

"Everyone should be home schooled" carries the same meaning as "I believe everyone should be home schooled." The reader is aware of the writer's point of view in the shortened thesis statement. So, eliminate first-person references, which often will introduce a slightly more difficult challenge to the student writer, one that will pay dividends as the student embarks on new adventures in writing other forms of fiction and non-fiction.

Assignment:

Remove first- and second-person references from your thesis statement. List three ways that you might be able to defend your thesis statement. Then begin gathering material that can be used to support these three points. You may wish to base some of your arguments on personal experience. You also should consider conducting research at a library, by surfing the Internet or by discussing the topic with other home school sources. This research may prompt you to revise the thesis statement and to alter the initial three arguments supporting your viewpoint.

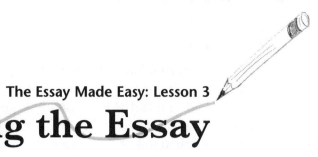

Organizing the Essay

The traditional essay is sometimes referred to as the five-paragraph essay: The introduction followed by three paragraphs of information and/or argumentation supporting the thesis statement and then the conclusion. Typically, each paragraph ranges in length from 200 to 300 words.

The writer paints with a broad brush in introducing the topic and concludes the first paragraph with the thesis statement, which is referred to as the focus or as the point of view.

In the five-paragraph essay, the strongest point supporting the thesis statement introduces the second paragraph. The other two points follow in separate paragraphs. The thesis statement introduces the final paragraph but is restated in a different form as the writer summarizes the arguments supporting the essay's point of view.

Assignment:

Before considering each of these parts of an essay, let's have some fun with a practice exercise:

1. Write three arguments in the form of topic sentences that support the following thesis statement: Summer is the most enjoyable season of the year.
2. Number your arguments beginning with the strongest.
3. Add one sentence of information that supports each of the three arguments.
4. Remember to avoid the use of first- or second-person in completing this exercise.

For your second assignment write three arguments in topic sentences that support the following thesis statement: Summer is the least enjoyable season of the year. Then add a sentence to each of the three arguments.

Note that you have argued in defense of and in opposition to the thesis statement. This process is the standard approach in conducting research for an essay. It helps ensure that the writer's viewpoints are valid and that concessions can be made in constructing an essay, a process that will be discussed in Lesson Six. More than three arguments may be offered in an essay by adding a paragraph for each argument. Keep in mind, however, that the attention span of the reading audience continues to grow shorter with each passing year. To attract and hold the reader's attention a writer must craft an interesting thesis statement and must present convincing arguments in a timely fashion. Our next task will be to write a compelling introduction.

Note to Teacher:

After the research has been completed, your student may wish to revise the following thesis statement: Everyone should be home schooled. You should act as an editor at this point and make certain the student 1) has a point of view that can be defended and 2) has gathered information that can be used for three arguments to support the thesis or point of view. The student should then follow the steps suggested in the exercises above and should turn in a written sentence outline for evaluation. You should note spelling and other errors and assign the student to rewrite the outline until it is acceptable.

Writing the Introduction

"I've finished my research, and I have changed my thesis statement," the student announces. "How do I write the introduction of my essay?"

Three steps: 1) begin the essay in an interesting manner, 2) preview your arguments and 3) conclude with your thesis statement.

In this case, the student has revised the original thesis of "Everyone should be home schooled" to "Children can receive a better education at home than in a public school." To support that viewpoint, the student has listed three arguments written as topic sentences in this order:

1. Students can receive individual attention and their classes can be tailored to their interests and needs.
2. Schooling at home can reduce peer pressure in classrooms and on the playground.
3. A number of resources are available to home school teachers and students.

The first impression is often the most important in any enterprise. The salesperson, for example, hopes to sell a service or a product. The job applicant wishes to be hired. The student hopes to receive a satisfactory grade. The essay writer wishes to capture the reader's interest, to hold the reader's attention until the final punctuation mark and to present a convincing argument.

Therefore, the first sentence should be crafted carefully and should give some hint about the essay's topic. The sentence should tease or whet the reader's curiosity. In the following example, the student takes the viewpoint of parents who decide to investigate home schooling for their son.

When the school district announced that first grade class sizes would be increased to 30 students rather than 20, John and Sarah Jones decided to investigate alternatives. They wondered whether their son, Jonathan, would receive any personal attention in a class that size. They also worried about peer pressure. Would Jonathan be tempted to do drugs? Would he be hassled or bullied on the playground? Would he be expected to wear certain kinds of clothing? Would he be expected to conform to behavior or be introduced to beliefs unacceptable to the family? Even though John and Sarah Jones had completed college, neither one felt qualified to teach. Their search, however, led them to a home school support group that promised help with selecting textbooks, study guides and other resources, including tutors and private educational centers. Armed with this information, John and Sarah Jones decided that their son could receive a better education at home than in a public school.

This 170-word paragraph serves as the first draft of the introduction. Note that the student writer's three arguments supporting the thesis statement are incorporated into the introduction. The arguments have been personalized. The reader can live the experience of the Jones family vicariously. Granted, the spelling of words will need to be checked. Some sentences may need to be revised. But the student has written an acceptable introduction.

Assignment:

Write the introduction to your essay. The paragraph should be 150 to 300 words in length. Turn in the first draft to your teacher for critiquing so that you can make corrections and can prepare a final draft of your paragraph. If you have access to a typewriter or to a computer, double space your lines. The student's name and the date the manuscript is written should always appear on the first page. In this case, the title of the essay should also appear. An example appears on the next page.

Student's full name
Month, day, year

Jonathan Doesn't "Catch the Bus"

When the school district announced that first grade class sizes would be increased to 30 students rather than 20, John and Sarah Jones decided to investigate alternatives. They wondered whether their son, Jonathan, would receive any personal attention in a class that size. They also worried about peer pressure. Would Jonathan be tempted to do drugs? Would he be hassled or bullied on the playground? Would he be expected to wear certain kinds of clothing? Would he be expected to conform to behavior or be introduced to beliefs unacceptable to the family? Even though John and Sarah Jones had completed college, neither one felt qualified to teach. Their search, however, led them to a home school support group that promised help with selecting textbooks, study guides and other resources, including tutors and private educational centers. Armed with this information, John and Sarah Jones decided that their son could receive a better education at home than in a public school.

The Essay Made Easy: Lesson 5

Building the Body

The middle section comprises the body of an essay and represents the arguments that support the thesis statement. The student's success in writing these three paragraphs in a five-paragraph essay will be determined in large part by his/her research. Facts, illustrations and the opinions of knowledgeable authorities come into play here. Without them, the writer often finds it difficult to produce 300 words per paragraph to support each of three arguments.

Fortunately, the student in the home school essay example discussed in the previous lesson has listed three satisfactory arguments in his/her outline and has referred to those points in the introductory paragraph.

The second essay paragraph should begin with the student's strongest argument, which is:

> Students can receive individual attention and their classes can be tailored to their interests and needs.

Note, however, that the student wrote the introduction from the viewpoint of John and Sarah Jones. To ensure what we refer to as a smooth transition from the introduction to the second paragraph, the writer should revise the first argument. For example, the student could introduce the second paragraph in this manner:

John and Sarah were confident that they could arrange their schedules to teach Jonathan and could tailor his home school instruction to meet his needs and interests.

At this point, the writer needs to expand that thought, to cite examples of how other home school parents have tailored instruction for their children. These examples could include how study periods were scheduled, where the instruction took place, how guidelines for classroom behavior were established. Ideally, the writer has gathered this information by talking to home school teachers or from other sources. The student could also develop this argument or topic sentence by making comparisons with public schools.

Assignment:

Write the second paragraph of your essay. It should be between 200 and 300 words. Make certain that your best argument appears in the first sentence in the paragraph. Turn in the first draft of your paragraph to your teacher for critiquing, which should be completed as soon as possible. Then rewrite the paragraph and repeat this process with the second and third paragraphs.

Note to Teacher:

This assignment will require more time than the previous ones. It is important, however, to encourage the student to complete this assignment as soon as possible. Students will find excuses for not conducting the research and for not completing the assignment. If you find the student balking at this point, the drill sergeant role might be the most appropriate teaching tool.

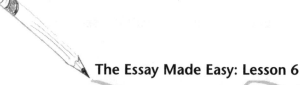

The Essay Made Easy: Lesson 6

Restating the Thesis

Writing the final paragraph of an essay often is the most difficult assignment. You are instructed to restate the thesis or focus in a slightly different form and to begin the final paragraph with that sentence.

Don't make this assignment unnecessarily difficult. Rephrasing the point you are attempting to make should be relatively easy. Then summarize the three arguments that you have presented earlier in the essay as convincingly as possible. Remember, you are repeating your arguments but you are using different words and examples to support them.

Restatement is the common and accepted practice in other forms of communication, including sermons, debates, editorials and non-fiction articles. Therefore, learning how to write the conclusion of an essay should serve you well as you explore other forms of writing.

Assignment:

Write the concluding paragraph of your essay. Like the introduction, it should be at least 150 words and not more than 300 words. Double space your lines. Turn in the first draft to your teacher for critiquing so that you can make corrections and can prepare a final draft of your paragraph.

Note to Teacher:

Most students will complain that they can't think of anything to write about in the conclusion, that 150 words are too many. You may need to show them how they can restate their arguments in a convincing manner. If you're looking for an example, explain what lawyers do when they make final statements to a jury. They draw on evidence and testimony offered earlier in the trial as they try to sway members of a jury to make a decision in favor of their client.

Transitions

Transitions are important linking devices in constructing an essay and in other forms of writing. For example: a newspaper reporter who properly constructs a feature story can defeat an editor's copy-cutting not only by arranging the building blocks properly, but also by incorporating transitional words and by linking thoughts from sentence to sentence and from paragraph to paragraph. Remove one of the building blocks, and the structure tumbles.

As a student, you probably are acquainted with mechanical transitions, which include: *therefore, moreover, clearly then, granted, on the other hand, in fact, nevertheless, thus, undoubtedly, yet*. Two other words should be used sparingly as transitional devices and a third should not be used to introduce a sentence. In the first instance, the conjunctions "and" and "but" are appearing more frequently at the beginning of a sentence. While the practice is gaining acceptance, it often indicates laziness on the part of the writer. The word "however" is best suited for use inside a sentence, not the beginning. Example: In his own words, however, he denied the charges. The rationale is based on sentence cadence. "However" seldom sounds right when leading a parade.

Several other types of transitions should be employed by writers, especially by beginners. By forming good writing habits, these linking devices eventually will appear naturally as a manuscript is being composed. The repetition of words, phrases and thoughts is one form. They need not be exact duplicates but may suggest the same meaning: tulip, flower, garden; or winter, snow, 30-degree weather. The principle also applies to the expression of a thought and then restating that thought in some other form in a later sentence(s) or paragraph(s).

Assignment:

Before copying or typing the final draft of your essay, underline transitional words, phrases and thoughts. Draw lines to show how they link sentences and paragraphs to one another. You may want to rewrite some sentences to incorporate these transitional devices. Before typing the final draft, however, read the next assignment in Lesson 8.

Note to Teacher:

If you are working with a student who is writing his/her first essay, you may want to skip this lesson and Lesson 8. Experience suggests that it is difficult to sustain interest in what students often perceive as a series of difficult research and writing assignments. It may be wise to turn to the series of simpler forms of essay writing that appear in Lessons 9 and 10. Then add Lessons 7 and 8 when the student writes the second point-of-view essay assignment in Lesson 11.

The Essay Made Easy: Lesson 8

Polishing the Product

The final step in the writing process involves revising and polishing the manuscript. You may want to put the essay aside for several days and let the manuscript "rest." Professional writers often follow this practice, one that brings a fresher perspective to the editing process. Then follow this checklist when evaluating your manuscript before turning in the final draft of your essay:

✓ Check the spelling of any word you are unsure of even though a computer program has been used to check spelling.

✓ Make certain that single antecedents match singular proper nouns and that verb tenses haven't been switched.

✓ Check every comma and be prepared to defend its use in a sentence.

✓ Rewrite any sentence that begins with the word "there." While "there" is a perfectly good word, writers discover that it should only be used in reference to place. Examples: "Place the book there," he said, motioning to the table. Otherwise, introducing an independent clause with *there* usually clutters a sentence and makes it sound stilted. Example:

There is a truck speeding down the road.
A truck speeds down the road.

There are 12 students in the room who are studying.
Twelve students study in the room.

Assignment:

Correct any errors and make any changes in the organization of your essay. Then turn in a double-spaced copy to your teacher. When the original is returned, make photocopies of the essay and share it with grandparents and with other members of your family. This is a form of being published and is important to your development as a writer. Then place one copy of your essay in your permanent writing file.

Note to Teacher:

You may wish to give the student a vacation break at this point in this writing curriculum. Lesson 9 is a miniature essay form that can be used for review. It will be a relatively easy assignment designed to jump start student interest in renewing *The Write Stuff Adventure*.

Letter to the Editor

A letter written to the editor of a newspaper normally appears in the editorial section. Because publications limit the length to 200 words or less, the letter should be organized as a super short essay.

It becomes imperative, therefore, that the writer has a well-defined viewpoint in an introductory paragraph and then supports that argument factually and logically.

Like the essay, a letter expressing an opinion should be introduced in an interesting manner. The circumstances or reasons for writing the letter must be mentioned and the writer's viewpoint expressed. All of that information might be presented in the first paragraph. An argument or two may then follow before the viewpoint is restated, usually in the final sentence.

In other words, the essay is stripped to its barest bones in constructing a letter to the editor.

Assignment:

This assignment may require two or more weeks to complete, depending on your class schedule. First, read several letters to the editor in your local newspaper. Note that they may vary in length and organization. Write a 25-word sentence expressing a viewpoint about some current issue of public concern to your community. Discuss this viewpoint, or thesis statement, with your teacher. Explain how you expect to support your viewpoint. When agreement is reached, write a letter of not more than 200 words to a newspaper editor. Revise the letter and prepare a final draft.

Note to Teacher:

Encourage the student to select a public issue and to write a short editorial comment about the issue for publication in a local newspaper. Help the student address an envelope to the publication's editorial page editor and submit the letter for publication. When the letter is printed, remove the entire page on which the letter appears from the publication and assign the student to place what is referred to as the "tear sheet" in his/her portfolio or permanent writing file. A byline or name in print can help motivate the student to continuing the writing adventure.

A Career Decision

You probably have some idea about what "I want to be when I grow up." Even though that decision is yet to be made and may be altered during a lifetime, a career offers a relatively simple topic for a writing exercise. It also gives you an opportunity to write in first person, to conduct a bit of research and to organize that material in an essay.

This author, for example, decided in a vague way that he wanted to be a journalist at the age of 5. That interest in writing was fostered by parents and grew through college. It led to a career as a writer and teacher and continues today, more than 60 years later. As a boy, I could have written an essay about my interest in becoming a writer. I could have listed at least three reasons why I thought I wanted to be a writer. Making money was not one of them. First and foremost, I was compelled to write by some inner drive. I wrote when I had a free moment. I liked to read words that I had written, and I felt that writing was valuable and worthwhile.

Research can take several forms. You may know someone who has followed a career of interest to you. Arrange to talk with that person and to include some of that person's experiences and thoughts in the essay. Read about historical figures who have followed such a career. What motivated those people? What were the challenges? What were the rewards? The Internet, of course, offers a wealth of statistical information about trades and professions, including career opportunities, income, and so on.

Assignment:

Write a 1,000-word essay in which you discuss a career that you may want to follow. The thesis statement can be some variation of: I want to be a (list the career/profession). List three reasons in topic sentences why you are interested in such a career in the order of their importance to you. Use each topic sentence to introduce paragraphs 2, 3 and 4. Restate your thesis and complete the fifth paragraph. Each paragraph should be at least 100 words. Double space your essay, place your name, the date the essay was written and the title of your essay at the top of the first page. Turn in the first draft of your essay to your teacher. When the draft is returned, correct errors and rewrite the essay. Place a copy of the final draft in your permanent writing file.

Note to Teacher:

Again, this assignment may require an extended length of time. It could be combined with with another segment of instruction that parallels the student's career interests or in the study of great people in history, literature, the Bible, etc. It is important, however, to maintain some sense of deadline in writing. So, set up deadlines for completing the research, turning in an outline of the thesis statement and topic sentences of an essay and submitting the first draft. Keep in mind that rewriting is important.

A Speech in the Making

No doubt you have heard a public speech or sermon. You may even have been assigned to write and to deliver a talk of some sort. These talks may have taken the form of a simple report about a 4-H project. Other talks may have been more formal. In any event, speeches usually are persuasive in nature. Have you noticed, for example, how your younger brother or sister offers an excuse for some behavior? They usually have a definite point of view and explain, defend or excuse such behavior, often what an adult may consider to be misbehavior. Such argumentation often is a mini-form of the point-of-view essay: I wanted the toy, my brother had it, he wouldn't give it to me, I took it, he ran crying to mother, etc.

On a more formal note, ministers often present what is referred to as a three-point sermon. The sermon is introduced in some interesting or compelling way, maybe with an anecdote, a humorous story or an illustration. This leads to the thesis statement, which is underscored by scripture. The three points support the thesis statement and comprise the bulk of the sermon. Finally, the minister restates the thesis and concludes the sermon.

Not all public speakers follow this form. Some deliver sound bites for television reporters. Others ramble. In an age of declining public interest in public debate and discourse of more than three minutes, it behooves speakers to be as organized and concise as possible. The essay represents an ageless vehicle for such a task.

Assignment:

Write a 1,000-word speech that you can deliver before some audience of your choice. Organize the speech as you would a point-of-view essay. Write the speech in the third person, which means that you are not to use *I, me, my* references. Complete your research, write a first draft and turn it in to your teacher. When it is returned, rewrite your essay and deliver the speech to members of your family or to friends. Place a copy in your permanent writing file.

Note to Teacher:

This assignment may require an extended period of time. It will provide an opportunity for the student to practice public speaking before a familiar and friendly audience. Provide some sort of podium upon which the student can place the speech.

Three suggestions: 1) The student should look briefly at the audience before beginning the speech, which he/she can read, 2) the student should not rush the delivery of the speech and 3) the student should not leave the speaking area until the speech has been delivered. When the speech is completed, for example, the student should look at the audience before being seated.

The student may find it helpful to practice delivering the speech in private several times. If you have a video camera or a tape recorder, record the formal presentation, which suggests to the student that what has been accomplished in *The Write Stuff Adventure* is worthwhile.

Another option for teachers who meet periodically with a home school group is to include this instruction in speech writing and presentation as a project. After the speeches have been written and presented at home, arrange for all students to deliver their speeches before the group of students and teachers.

An Essay with Concessions

Concessions often can strengthen an argument. By admitting that the opposition may have contrary arguments of merit, your audience may be impressed with the scope of your research and you often can use the concession as a strawman. In other words, you make a concession and then topple it with a stronger argument.

A concession may introduce a paragraph or it may stand alone in a separate paragraph. Most writers prefer to limit the concession. For example:

> Granted, more than 90 percent of all children attend public schools in the United States. Numbers alone, however, do not reflect the quality of educa-tion. A national report shows that home school children rank among the high-est in test scores…

Note that mechanical transitions often are important in setting off a concession and in transitioning to a topic sentence.

In this final project, you are assigned to include concessions in the essay.

Assignment:

Pick a thesis statement based on a subject that you are studying or on a public issue. Your thesis statement of 25 words or less should express a point of view. Remember, you are not writing a report. Research your viewpoint and list three arguments that support it. Also list three arguments that oppose your viewpoint.

Organize your essay in this manner:

✓ Introduction, which summarizes the arguments you will use in the body of your essay. Conclude with your thesis statement.

✓ Introduce the first paragraph with a concession or opposing viewpoint to your strongest argument. Transition to your strongest argument.

✓ Organize your third and fourth paragraphs in the same manner.

✓ Introduce your fifth and final paragraph with your thesis statement. Make certain, however, that you have rephrased that statement so that it is not the exact duplication of the thesis you used to end the first paragraph. Broaden your conclusion by summarizing your three arguments.

✓   The introduction and conclusion should be at least 200 words and not more than 300 words.

✓   Paragraphs two, three and four should be in the 300-word range.

✓   Don't forget to include your name, the date the essay was completed and a title on the first page of your manuscript.

✓   Before turning in the essay to your teacher, underline transitional words and thoughts. You may need to make changes to ensure that transitions appear throughout your essay.

✓   After your teacher critiques your work, make corrections and changes in writing a final draft. Turn in this draft to your teacher. Place a copy in your permanent writing file.

✓   It's time to celebrate. At this point you have completed the foundation upon which all writing is constructed. You have taken an important step in *The Write Stuff Adventure*.

Note to Teacher:

Award the student a gold star, a certificate of completion or some form of recognition. Sharing copies of the essay with members of the extended family and friends often is a reward worth considering. Or publish all of the student's essays completed during this study. Invite the student to design a cover, make photocopies and staple the booklet. Then distribute copies to members of the extended family and friends. For those teachers who are members of a home school group that meets with students periodically, the work of students who are studying essay writing can be published as a class project.

Section Four:

Interviewing and the Non-Fiction Article

Note to Teacher

You run down the trail, dodging branches and jumping over roots. Adrenaline rushes through your veins as you sprint around a bend and hopscotch past puddles.

Deer tracks dot the path, but that's not what you're after today. You're hunting for the opposing team's flag, which is somewhere up ahead, enveloped in the woods.

You hear a twig snap, and the bushes rustle up ahead beside the trail. You draw your gun, drop to the ground and roll under the low-lying branches of a small tree.

A camouflaged figure steps warily out from behind a thick fir, gun held ready in hand and wearing a khaki-green facemask. He scopes the trail, turns and proceeds toward you, bending low as he jogs. One of the opponents, you know, from the color of his armband.

Your heart throbs as you ready your gun.[6]

This introduction to a paintball story was written by a 16-year-old home school student enrolled in the *Write Stuff* program in 1995. The story was published by *The Register-Guard* daily newspaper in Eugene, Oregon.

Non-fiction articles like this one represent a staple in our reading diet. Newspapers, magazines and other publications publish what is referred to as feature stories that provide information about interesting people, places and things. The subject matter ranges from humorous to serious. While the feature article may be related to some important event or issue, it is structured more like an essay than a news story. Therefore, learning how to organize and write a feature article is the next logical step in *The Write Stuff Adventure*.

The art of interviewing will be explored in more depth as the study begins. Students will be expected to move outside comfortable family surroundings to gather information. It will, however, offer an opportunity for students to become better acquainted with the world in which they live under the watchful eye of a parent/teacher. Several suggestions will be offered, including how to take notes and how to use a tape recorder.

Several writing exercises are included to help the student understand story organization. The student then graduates to gathering information, organizing his notes and writing three feature articles. The first two articles require that the student interview a single source. The third requires the student to decide what to write about and who to interview. En route to this destination, the student will review anecdotes and study markets, a term that refers to places that might publish a feature article.

---

6. Written by Mario Currado, a home school student.

The teacher serves as an editor during this study. The student will be expected to write and submit a first draft of an assignment to the teacher, who will return it with suggested changes. The teacher/editor should note, but not correct, misspelled words and problems with punctuation, syntax (sentence construction), transitions and story organization. Offer suggestions but don't do the student's work. Rewriting a first draft should require more than copying the teacher/editor's editing changes. Don't hesitate to require more than one revision of an assignment. Granted, this may slow the process, but the objective is to help the writer learn and polish language skills.

The student should avoid writing in first person until he/she becomes acquainted with and has completed several feature articles. The student should strive to write in what is referred to as non-person. In other words, the writer should not introduce his/her feelings or evaluations. Report the information, opinions and observations of other sources, including those you meet in conducting library research and in personal interviews.

Publication is important. While initial efforts may not merit publication in a newspaper, magazine or newsletter, copies of the student's final draft of the three essays assigned in this study can be shared with members of the extended family and friends. Design a cover page that includes a generic title, a brief description of the project and the student's name. The second article about a person's favorite recipe(s) may be accepted by a local newspaper, especially if it's a small daily or weekly. Again, publication is a reward that helps motivate a student to participate in *The Write Stuff Adventure*.

Common Factors

The progression from essay writing to feature writing is a natural one for most writers. Awaiting them is an organizational form that is a close relative of the essay. To begin, envision the feature as a five-paragraph essay. The feature writer needs a focus statement and information to support it. As soon as the focus or point of the story is introduced, the writer needs to present three or four points that support the focus, then close with a restatement of the focus. Granted, the paragraphs of the feature are shorter and more numerous, but the two forms are closely related.

"A feature story evolves, when to make a point, the writer controls the facts by selection, structure and interpretation rather than the facts controlling the writer," writes Kenneth Metzler in his book, *Newsgathering.*[7]

"The feature is a long, nonfiction story, 800 to 3,000 or more words, written in clear, simple language and dressed out rather casually," writes Vicky Hay in her book, *The Essential Feature.*[8]

Hay goes on to say that the feature article "resembles a newspaper story in that it is always factual and its writer is expected to adhere to high standards of accuracy and honesty…But unlike a news story, it begins with a lead like a fictional opening and presents facts in a more flexible manner."

Several types of stories are referred to as features. The human-interest feature shares something interesting about an individual. Celebrity stories often fit this category. Some features investigate social, political, economic and other public issues. Whatever the category, the feature writer looks for, finds and writes a story based on facts, a story that offers a bit of reality for readers that may not be found in news stories.

An Example:

The following paragraphs written about a game of paintball introduce what is called a feature or non-fiction article. After the introduction, the author presented the story focus:

> You run down the trail, dodging branches and jumping over roots. Adrenaline rushes through your veins as you sprint around a bend and hopscotch past puddles.

---

7. Kenneth Metzler, *Newsgathering* (Englewood, Cliffs, NJ: Prentice-Hall, Inc., 1979), 190.
8. Vicky Hay, *The Essential Feature* (New York: Columbia University Press), 8.

Deer tracks dot the path, but that's not what you're after today. You're hunting for the opposing team's flag, which is somewhere up ahead, enveloped in the woods.

You hear a twig snap, and the bushes rustle up ahead beside the trail. You draw your gun, drop to the ground and roll under the low-lying branches of a small tree.

A camouflaged figure steps warily out from behind a thick fir, gun held ready in hand and wearing a khaki-green facemask. He scopes the trail, turns and proceeds toward you, bending low as he jogs. One of the opponents, you know, from the color of his armband.

Your heart throbs as you ready your gun.

After the introduction, the author presented the story focus:

Looking for something new to spice up your summer? You might want to try the action-paced, adrenaline-pumping game of paintball, which is a glorified game of tag.

It would have been difficult to write a news story based on the information in this paintball story because there was nothing "new" to report. As a feature, however, the writer was able to explain why paintball is a popular way to beat the summer doldrums, how it is played, how much it costs and who plays the game.

Assignment:

Look through a daily newspaper and identify five news stories and five feature articles. Discuss them with your home school teacher. Be prepared to explain why you believe these stories are either news stories or feature articles. Here are some tips that will help you identify news stories: 1) They often report important and timely events, and 2) they often introduce the 5 Ws and the H (who, when, what, where, why and how) in the first two or three paragraphs of the story. The feature writer may set the scene or tell a short story in the first few paragraphs before introducing the focus of the article.

Note to Teacher:

Paragraphs in news and feature stories traditionally are 25 to 35 words in length. The rationale is that newspaper and magazine writers are quickly discouraged by long sentences and paragraphs. So, these writers "break up the gray type" by writing tightly and by sprinkling direct quotes throughout a story. Also note that the conclusion of a feature article may consist of a paragraph or two in which the writer uses a direct quote or summarizes the point of the story with an anecdote. This is referred to as a "kicker," which will be discussed in more detail in later lessons.

Quotes, Notes, Anecdotes

Quotes

Three housekeeping items need to be reviewed before we resume our study of interviewing: quotes, notes and anecdotes.

Most of you have learned how to use quotation or quote marks. The most frequent use of this punctuation in feature writing is to set off or identify words that are quoted verbatim.

Two matters of style are important in writing features and, as we will learn later, in writing news stories.

✓ The period or comma always appears inside the closed quotation marks at the end of the quotation.

✓ Slang words and phrases are not set off or placed inside quotation marks.

Beginning students frequently are confused about what to do with punctuation when a source is added to a sentence. Here are examples of the correct way to punctuate what writers refer to as attribution:

"The writer is an artisan and should strive to excel," she said.

She said, "The writer is an artisan and should strive to excel."

"The writer is an artisan," she said, "and should strive to excel."

The writer uses four types of quoted material: direct, indirect, modified and paraphrase. Examples follow:

Direct quote:

A direct quotation is used to report the verbatim comment or the exact words of some person. The direct quotation is placed inside quotation marks.

Example: "I was so nervous while interviewing the mayor that my knees and my pencil had the wobbles," he said.

Indirect quote:

The speaker's ideas are presented mainly but not entirely in his/her own words.Quotation marks are not used.

Example: He said he was so nervous interviewing the mayor that his knees and pencil were shaking.

Modified quotation:

Using a portion of direct quotation in a sentence is referred to as modified quotation.

Example: He said he was so nervous interviewing the mayor that his knees and pencil "had the wobbles."

Paraphrase:

In paraphrase, the writer uses his/her own words rather than the words of the speaker. Paraphrase often permits shortening the direct quotation and may clarify the statement. Again, no quote marks are used.

Example: He said he was nervous while interviewing the mayor.

Assignment:

Find examples in a publication of direct, indirect, modified quotation and paraphrase. Note that the source of each statement should be included in the sentence, which is referred to as attribution. (Including attribution is important to feature and news writers.)

Taking Notes

As we mentioned in an earlier *Write Stuff* study, taking full-sentence notes is important in gathering information, especially if the writer expects to quote a source verbatim.

Guidelines:

- ✓ Take notes on only one side of a sheet of paper. This practice will facilitate the organization of notes while the story is being written.

- ✓ On the first page of your notes, identify your source (Example: the name of the person interviewed). Include the month, day and year the notes were recorded.

- ✓ Number the pages of your notes.

- ✓ Keep your notes until after the story is published so that you can check information.

✓ Make certain that names and places are spelled correctly. Don't assume, for example, that a person with the last name of Smith follows the common spelling of that word. It may be spelled Smythe.

Assignment:

Practice taking notes while listening to a speech delivered during some public event or broadcast on radio or on television. Then copy five full-sentence quotes on a separate sheet of paper and turn in the assignment to your teacher. Discuss difficulties you encountered in taking notes and how you might improve your skills through practice.

The Anecdote

You may recall that we collected stories about members of the family during our study of personal and family history. We learned that an anecdote is something that can be used to illustrate a point in a story. An anecdote is sometimes referred to as a short, short story. It is a valuable tool for writers, especially those who wish to show rather than to tell readers something about a subject. For example, the writer may tell readers that a child is kind to pets. It would be more effective and interesting, however, to share an incident about how that child showed kindness to a pet. The latter is an anecdote. Gathering such stories is an important part of an interview.

Assignment:

Read a magazine article. If you find an anecdote, share it with your teacher.

Note to Teacher:

In a later lesson students will be required to obtain an anecdote while interviewing a source. Suggestions will be offered on how to obtain an anecdote and how to use it in writing a feature.

The Art of Interviewing

"What time is it?" the student asks.

"Two o'clock," the parent answers.

"Can I quit practicing the piano now?"

"No."

"But I'm hungry. Can I have something to eat?"

While the answers to these questions are direct and often yes or no responses, the student in this example is gathering information in a conversation with another person. This simple form of interviewing normally is friendly and non-threatening.

The scene changes, however, when a student is assigned to gather information by talking to a stranger. The student often becomes nervous, even terrified. This same student may be undaunted and unafraid to surf the Internet or to seek information in a library. Despite the panic that interviewing often creates among beginners, it is a craft and eventually an art that writers should master, including those who create fiction.

Preparation and practice are keys to relieving stress in interviewing another person, who is called the respondent. The student, for example, can prepare by:

✓ Acquiring background information on the topic of the feature article.

✓ Preparing a topic statement that is expected to be the focus of the story.

✓ Knowing something about the respondent being interviewed.

✓ Writing a list of questions to ask.

✓ Making an appointment to interview the respondent.

✓ Rehearsing the interview with some other person such as the home school teacher.

Interviewing involves learning the tools of the craft. In the beginning, all sorts of things can go wrong. The student can be so nervous that he/she fails to clarify the purpose of the interview with the respondent. The student may find it difficult to take notes. The interview session may be interrupted by outside distractions. Maybe the conversation goes well, but the student later is unable to recall details and has no direct quotes for use in writing the feature.

With practice, the student will become skilled at the art of interviewing. The student who bumbles through a first interview may have to return for a second, even a third, before acquiring the necessary information. Confidence grows with each interview, and before the study of feature writing ends, the student should be a still-somewhat-nervous but successful interviewer.

Assignment:

Visit one of the following places. Identify yourself as a student who is learning how to interview people. Do not attempt to take notes. Write a 200-word report on what you remember about the interview and discuss the interview with your teacher.

1. Visit a local car dealership. Ask a salesperson how to sell a car.

2. Visit a library. Ask a librarian what makes the job interesting.

3. Visit a church and talk to a minister. Ask how the minister prepares a sermon.

4. Visit a pet store. Ask an employee what pets are the most popular and why.

5. Visit a neighbor. Ask the neighbor to tell you about the most exciting thing that happened during his/her childhood.

Note to Teacher:

Use the terms interviewer and respondent when discussing this subject with your student. The objective of this assignment is to begin building the student's confidence in his/her ability to meet and talk face-to-face with people outside the family about a specific topic. These respondents may be acquaintances but should not be close friends. The interview may be no more than a brief conversation with the respondent. Use the written report as a confidence-builder. Look for things to praise, things that might prompt a discussion about the interview. Remember, we're involved in an adventure. It may be work, but it should be adventuresome work that is filled with fun.

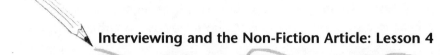

Do You Have Questions?

Now that you have interviewed either a car salesperson, a librarian, a minister, a pet store worker or a neighbor, it is time to conduct a second interview. This one will be more interesting. Here's the report that you, the student, hear:

A 14-year-old boy who lives in your neighborhood has turned a hobby of photography into a part-time business. This information isn't news because most everyone in the neighborhood knows that Jimmy Jones has been taking photographs for years. It is information that might, however, be developed into a feature article, maybe a story that the local daily newspaper would publish on its "teen" page.

Assignment:

1. Based on the information about the boy photographer above, decide what the focus of your article will be and write a sentence of not more than 25 words similar to a thesis statement for an essay. Remember, however, that you are not expected to write a point-of-view essay. Rather, the feature article is told in a more informal manner and may be entertaining as well as informative. Your objective is to write a factual article that will interest newspaper readers of all ages.

2. Write five questions that you can ask the respondent, Jimmy Jones, about his hobby. Avoid questions that Jimmy can answer with a simple "yes" or "no." Phrase questions so that he will explain the hobby, why it interests him and how he goes about taking pictures.

3. If you are unfamiliar with photography, conduct a bit of research in the library or on the Internet.

4. Discuss your focus statement and questions with your teacher.

Note to Teacher:

This exercise will be continued in the next lesson. Remind the student that the focus sentence or thesis statement may change after Jimmy is interviewed. The student may unearth interesting information that may suggest a new focus.

It is important, too, for the student to begin thinking about asking "open-ended" questions that invite the respondent to make a statement rather than to give simply a "yes" or "no" response. Examples of yes-no questions: Do you enjoy taking pictures? Do you use more than one camera? Examples of questions that invite full-sentence responses. Tell me what you enjoy about taking pictures. Describe your favorite camera and tell me why you like it. (Note that the latter examples are really not stated as questions but as invitations to share information, opinions, insights, etc.)

With the focus statement and the list of questions, the student is prepared to arrange and to conduct an interview, which will be discussed in the next lesson.

Answers to Your Questions

"I've got my focus sentence and five questions," the student says. "Now, what do I do?"

Make an appointment to talk person-to-person with Jimmy Jones, who lives at 1230 Tinkertown Road. His parents are Bill and Susie Jones. Their telephone number is 687-9234.

Before you make the appointment, however, check your calendar and settle on two or three times that you would be available to conduct the interview. Also practice what you will say when Jimmy answers the telephone.

- ✓ Tell him your name and why you are calling: "My name is Dean Rea and I would like to talk to you about your hobby of photography. What time would be best for me to talk with you at your home? I would like to see your cameras and some of your photographs so that I can write an article."

- ✓ Make certain that you arrive on time for the interview. One of your parents may want to accompany you to Jimmy's house. Maybe one or both of Jimmy's parents are there, too. After introductions, explain that you want to be alone with Jimmy while you are interviewing him. (Insist on privacy. Otherwise, you'll be interrupted and you will be unable to concentrate on asking questions and taking notes of what Jimmy says.)

- ✓ Take along two pencils, a note pad and your questions.

- ✓ Before asking your questions, however, take a look at photographs Jimmy has taken and at his cameras and other photographic equipment. Interviewers call this "setting the scene." You get to know Jimmy. He gets to know you. Explain again the purpose of the interview. You want to know about his hobby.

- ✓ Now, you can begin asking your five questions. Write his responses on your note pad. Don't worry about spelling. Remember to write on only one side of a sheet of paper. If Jimmy speaks too fast, ask him to repeat his answer. If you are unsure whether you have quoted Jimmy correctly, repeat what you have written. Remember that it is important to record several verbatim (direct) quotes that you can use in writing a feature article.

- ✓ You discover while looking through Jimmy's work that a photograph of an accident involving a car and a truck won a blue ribbon at the county fair. How did he happen to take the photograph? Jimmy's answer may suggest other questions that you should ask before moving on to one of your prepared questions.

✓ You learn through those questions that Jimmy sold the car and truck accident photograph for $25 to the local daily newspaper and that he once earned $100 for taking photographs of a wedding. Eventually, you learn that he plans to attend college and become a professional photographer.

✓ Maybe you don't ask all of the five questions on your list because you have based most of your questions on what Jimmy tells you about his hobby. One of the questions on your list is important, you believe, so you ask who Jimmy's favorite photographer is and why.

✓ End the interview by thanking Jimmy for taking the time to meet with you. Tell him that you may want to check with him later about information in your notes and ask when you can call him on the telephone.

✓ Return home and review your notes. Incomplete notes should be written out at this time. If you have time, prepare a short outline of your article.

Note to Teacher:

Share the notes (on the following page) that were taken by a writer who interviewed Jimmy Jones about his hobby. Some notes are phrases. Some words are misspelled. Quotation marks appear around direct (verbatim) quotes. The interviewer's questions normally do not appear as part of the notes. Assign the student to read the following notes and then discuss them with him or her. Point out that notes usually contain incomplete sentences, misspelled words and abbreviations.

Respondent: Jimmy Jones
Date of Interview

lives at 1230 Tinkertown Road.

He's 6 feet tall, 14 years old, in eighth grade, parents Bill and Susie Jones, no brothers or sisters. He has turned his hobby of photography into a part-time business.

"Yeah, ive been taking pictures since I was 7. Got a camera for Christmas that year and sorta got into it."

hasn't taken any classes. Self taught. Won a blue ribbon at the county fair when he was 10. "The photo was of a car-truck accident that I shot just as the accident occurd. I was starting to take a photo of a man across the street when the accident happnd. I just reacted. Got a great pictgure that the local newspaper printed. Gave me $25 for it."

"I decided then that I mite make some $ with my camera so I started looking for jobs. Got to take a wedding when I was 12. The official photogrpher didn't show up. I had my camera bag. Got $100 for that job."

He has two cameras, a 35 mm Nikon with four lenses and a 2 1/4 x 2 1/4 Mamiya. Both were used when he bot them. Has about $1000 in them. Also has a flash. Likes to take black and white photos but doesn't like to develop and print them in his home darkroom. Prefers to take color and have it developed and printed commercially.

He now takes pictures at every opportunity. Attends school social functions, takes pictures of athletes in action at his school. Takes photos of any group that might like to buy a print.

"I went to a square dance festival and snapped photos of every group there. I must have taken two or three rolls. I hand out cards with my name, address and phone number on it. But I've found it is better to get the money right on the spot. Its hard to sell later."

He plans to attend a college that has a good photo program and wants to be a magazine photographer, maybe for National Geographic.

He recalls one incident where he nearly lost his camera and his life. "I was taking photographs of the high school senior class and decided to get above the group. So, I got on the roof of the gym and leaned over the side. I must have been 100 feet or so in the air. Just as I started to take the first picture, I slipped and fell. I caught the ledge but my camera plunged toward the ground. Fortunately, it was on a strap around my neck and wasn't damaged."

Advice to beginners: "learn the craft. practice, practice, practice. look for new opportunities. dare to take calculated risks. don't overcharge for your work. dont be afraid to talk to people."

Has he made any money? "Well, yes and no. I've about paid for my cameras and equipment, Its hard to take much money when you only charge a couple of dollars for a 5x7. I guess I should charge more but right now I like to share my work with others. and I'd rather be able to sell my photographs than just to take them as a hobby and paste them in an album that nobody ever sees."

His favorite photogapher? "I like the work of Ansel Adams. He did a lot of still life, some people. But I'm more into action stuff. I suppose I prefer photographers who concentrate on people. They're alive. Thats what I want my photographs to be. Alive."

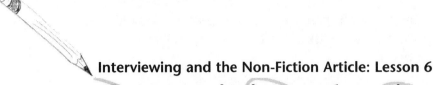

Organizing the Article

If we use the essay as a model for writing the feature article, the introduction should be interesting and it should end by announcing the point of the story. We then need to offer information in the body of the story that supports this particular focus. While the essay serves as an organizational model, the feature writer is at liberty to be more informal in presenting material.

First, paragraphs usually contain one to three sentences. The length of the sentences may vary. For example, the first paragraph in "The Sound of Water" illustration that appears at the end of this lesson is six words long.

Second, the introduction may consist of several paragraphs leading up to the point of the story, which you will note in reading the two examples at the end of this lesson.

The writer may wish to set the scene as a movie often does in the opening minutes of the film. Or the writer may tell an anecdote or concentrate on some interesting or unusual incident to gain the reader's attention. Seldom does the writer begin a feature story with a direct quotation or with a question. Numerous other options exist.

After the story is introduced, the writer should select facts, examples, statements by authorities and other materials that support the point of the story. This selection process is as important in feature writing as it is in essay writing. Keep in mind that the writer probably has collected more material from library research and from interviews than can possibly fit into an 800- to 1,000-word article. It is often difficult to persuade a beginning writer to discard some of his/her precious information. But selection is important.

A rule-of-thumb followed by some writers is to introduce a direct quote after the introductory section and to sprinkle direct quotes throughout the remainder of the article. Beginners, however, often are unable to write down full-sentence direct quotes during the interview that illustrate points they want to make in the article. That problem can be corrected with practice.

Feature writers also attempt to obtain a direct quote, an anecdote or material that will restate the point of the story for use in writing a conclusion. Unlike the essay, the conclusion of a feature may be a direct quote, an anecdote or some other form of summing up the point of the story in what is called a "kicker."

Assignment:

You and your teacher have two assignments in this lesson.

1. Each of you is to find two examples of feature stories in a newspaper or magazine and to share them with each other. Underline the focus statement in the introduction and in the conclusion.

2. Study the following examples of how writers have introduced and concluded feature stories.

The Sound of Water

By Scotta Callister

The ever-changing sound of moving water.
The reflection of summer skies on quiet water.
The chatter of birds drawn to the shallows, and the splash of a leaping frog.
For these reasons and more, *Keizer residents are dipping their toes into the enjoyable world of water gardening.* And that's a big world, ranging from simple table-top bowl arrangements to ponds and streams that can dominate a yard.

(conclusion)

Baker (one of the sources quoted in the article) *recommends water features for anyone who would like a little buffer from the hustle and bustle of city or suburban life.* In her own yard, a large pond—complete with a waterfall, frogs and fish—provides a little serenity for both eyes and ears.
"We can't hear the traffic, the neighbors," she said. "And it's very relaxing just to come out and work around it in the yard."[8]

Sorority Cooking

By Jaime Lyn Rea

A dark-haired cook, dressed in jeans and a T-shirt, adds a little of this and a little of that to the creamy mixture in the metal pot sitting on the General Electric stove. She stirs the concoction with a wire whisk. The cook dips a spoon gingerly into the large pot and samples the rich sauce. "It's a little salty," she says, "but when the meat is added it will be okay.

"I've always liked cooking," says the 33-year-old cook, Debbie Skipper, a resident of Eugene, Oregon. When she was a girl, her grandmother taught her to cook. Even though she was involved in 4-H and baked for and entered many fairs, she says, "I never won anything."

---

8. *Keizertimes*, Keizer, Ore., May 1, 1997.

As the years have gone by *she has developed a love for cooking*. She likes it well enough to cook for the 50 members of Delta Delta Delta, or Tri Delta, a University of Oregon sorority.

(conclusion)

"I never get tired of cooking," Skipper says. She was delighted recently to create a new casserole for the women. She had fake crab, cocktail shrimp, white sauce and some vegetables in the refrigerator, so she mixed the ingredients together with pasta and seasonings and created Confetti Seafood Alfredo, a casserole that many of the young women enjoyed so much that there were hardly any leftovers.[9]

Note to Teacher:

In identifying and sharing feature stories with your student, keep in mind that some news stories are introduced much like features, which may make it difficult to differentiate between the two. Normally, most of the 5Ws and the H will appear early in the news story. The distinction will become clearer if the student studies news writing later in Section Five.

The "Sound of Water" and "Sorority Cooking" illustrate ways that writers have introduced and ended feature articles. The focus of each article appears in the paragraph that ends the introduction. That focus is restated in different terms in the conclusion. Everything that appears in the middle section should explain, support and relate to the focus statement.

---

9. Written by Jaime Lyn Rea, a home school student.

The Jimmy Jones Story

Now that we have a general idea about how to organize and write a feature article, let's return to the Jimmy Jones notes in Lesson 5. Our objective is to use that information to write a feature article.

Assignment:

Re-read the notes in Lesson 5 from the interview with Jimmy Jones about his photography hobby.

Your first assignment is to decide on a focus and to write it in the form of a sentence. Then write an introduction that is two or more paragraphs long. The focus statement should appear in the last paragraph of the introduction. Remember that paragraphs in feature stories usually contain one to three sentences that are often only 35 to 50 words long. Some are even shorter. Write your name at the top of the first page and double space the article. Have your teacher critique your introduction before writing the body and conclusion.

Some of the Jimmy Jones notes are phrases that will need to be made into sentences. A number of words are misspelled. Remember that direct quotes appear inside quotation marks in the notes. You can change any of them to indirect quotes or paraphrase them.

Turn in a rough draft of the entire story to your teacher, who will critique your article. Then write a second draft and place it in your permanent writing file.

Note to Teacher:

This assignment may be difficult because the student didn't conduct the interview and will not be personally acquainted with the respondent. On the other hand, the student has more information available than most first-time interviewers would have recorded.

The student is a gatekeeper of information in that he/she decides what information to use and how best to attract the reader's attention in the introduction. In other words, the student may decide to begin by telling about Jimmy's prize-winning photograph of the car and truck accident and how that led to his choice of a hobby and maybe a career. Or the writer might begin with the wedding or with a description of Jimmy's cameras. Other writers might begin with the anecdote about Jimmy nearly falling while taking the senior high photographs.

If the focus or point of the story is that Jimmy Jones has developed a hobby into a part-time business, several examples appear in the notes that can be developed into the body of the feature article. As in an essay, the more interesting or significant examples should appear early in the middle section.

The conclusion could consist of Jimmy's advice to beginners or his wanting to be like his favorite photographer, the late Ansel Adams, by taking pictures of people.

Encourage your student's attempt at organizing and writing this feature story. If organization is a problem, suggest that the student number sections of the notes and assemble the story that way. If the student has problems introducing the story, suggest that he/she pick a paragraph that illustrates the focus statement.

After the first draft is turned in, you might share the following examples of how other writers might have introduced the story.

Examples of introductions that end with the focus sentence:

The photograph Jimmy Jones took of a car and truck accident when he was 10 years old not only won a blue ribbon in the county fair, but also earned $25 after it was published in the local newspaper.

"I was starting to take a photo of a man across the street when the accident happened," Jimmy said. "I just reacted."

The photograph is one of many that the 14-year-old eighth grader has taken during the last seven years. During that time, his hobby has turned into a part-time business.

* * *

Jimmy Jones recalls the day he nearly lost his camera and his life.

"I was taking photographs of the high school senior class and decided to get above the group. So, I got on the roof of the gym and leaned over the side.

"I must have been 100 feet or so in the air. Just as I started to take the first picture, I slipped and fell. I caught the ledge, but my camera plunged toward the ground. Fortunately, it was on a strap around my neck and wasn't damaged."

Jimmy, a 14-year-old eighth grader, said he has been taking photographs since he was 7 years old, and he's considering photography as a career.

Interviewing and the Non-Fiction Article: Lesson 8

Getting an Anecdote

Students often write about their favorite topics. It's a win-win situation because beginners normally can be enticed to write about something they like, especially if no research is involved. So, the student writes something like this: "My dog minds real well."

Now, that sentence is a real grabber, isn't it? Something only a mother can love, especially if the student has balked at writing and has finally demonstrated that "yes, Johnny or Jenny can write."

The next step, and one that can begin to make writing an adventure, is to invite you, the student, to explain how the dog behaves "real well." For example, you might write: "My dog sits when I tell it to sit and will sit there for hours unless I tell it to do something else. I remember the time when I told Old Spot to sit and a cat he usually chases ran by. He wanted to chase that cat so bad every muscle in his body was quivering, but he never moved until I told him to."

What you have shared is an anecdote, which is defined as "a story within a story" by the Missouri Group in a book titled, *Beyond the Inverted Pyramid*. "It may help to set a scene or to reveal the character of a person or a place. It may be used as a lead or in the body of the story.[10]

Kenneth Metzler in his book, *Creative Interviewing*, defines an anecdote as "a factual storiette that illustrates a point." He notes that nonfiction writers who illustrate their points with interesting anecdotes accomplish three things: Their writing is more believable, it's more interesting and "readers identify with characters and episodes in anecdotes, comparing them to their own experiences."[11]

In the example above, you have used an anecdote, or a super-short story, to illustrate how well Old Spot behaves, which is much more interesting to read and to write than to say that "my dog minds real well."

The trick, of course, is to gather anecdotes that can be used in writing an article. Anecdotes often are shared in normal conversation between members of the family and friends. They also can be gathered during interviews, especially if the writer wishes to "show" rather than to "tell."

The next step in learning how to interview, therefore, involves gathering anecdotes.

11. The Missouri Group, *Beyond the Inverted Pyramid* (New York: St. Martin's Press, 1993), 36.
12. Kenneth Metzler, *Creative Writing* (Boston: Allyn and Bacon, 1997), 106-107.

Assignment:

Interview an adult, who can be a member of your family, about some subject. During the interview, strive to obtain two anecdotes that will tell your readers something about that person, who is the respondent.

Example:

My father enjoys football and often cheers when "little players" score or make a big play during a game. During an interview I asked him questions about why he cheers these players. My father, who is 5-foot-2, tells the following story:

"I guess I cheer for the little guy because I was little when I went to high school."

The high school only had 100 students enrolled. It was in Ohio.

"I was really too small to play football, but I could run. Actually, I only weighed 125 pounds. The only position open was halfback. We had guys big enough to play that position but they refused. So, I volunteered and played two years."

Dad lettered both years and was co-captain his senior year. The team won two games but lost 16.

"Sure, I got creamed a lot of the time, but I was fast and that's the way I stayed alive," he said.

Take notes during your interview. Strive to take verbatim quotes, especially when recording an anecdote. You can ask your respondent to speak slowly, even to repeat a statement for you.

Your report should:

1. List the first and last name of your respondent and include the time and date of the interview on the first page of your notes.

2. Identify anecdote No. 1 and anecdote No. 2. Your notes should also contain other information obtained during the interview.

3. Take notes on only one side of a sheet of paper.

4. Turn in your notes and discuss the anecdotes with the teacher.

Note to Teacher:

The student will be more comfortable interviewing a parent or members of the extended family who have shared experiences during conversations that can be fleshed out during an interview. These interviews often turn up a gold mine of anecdotes. Encourage the student to continue asking questions during the interview, seeking details about experiences that a parent shares. Encourage him or her to interview the person face-to-face in private. No one else should be present during the interviews assigned as part of *The Write Stuff Adventure*.

Remind the student that it is okay to misspell words, to abbreviate words and to write incomplete sentences while taking notes. The objective is to record as much information as possible. Quotation marks should be used, however, to indicate verbatim statements in notes. It often is helpful for interviewers, especially beginners, to look at their notes immediately after the interview and to make additions and changes. Students should be encouraged to trust their memories but not for too long a time before adding to their notes or before writing the story.

The student may be able to obtain only one anecdote. That's worth applauding.

Featuring the News

This is an optional assignment which will 1) offer you practice in writing a short feature article and 2) show how a news story can be featurized.

A newspaper published the following news story:

> Firefighters used chisels yesterday afternoon to free an 8-year-old boy who was stuck in the chimney at his home at 503 E. Vermont St.

> Andy Brown, son of Bill and Nancy Brown, told firemen he found the door locked when he got home from school and decided to climb down the chimney to get in the house.

> The boy's only injury was a chipped tooth, firemen said.

In this example, the reporter based the news story on a brief written report in the fire department office. The reporter had a writing deadline to meet and did not have time to interview the boy, the parents or the firemen.

If the reporter had been able to conduct these interviews, the following information might have been uncovered from the written report at the fire station. You can attribute this information to firefighters but none of it is direct quotation. So, don't add quotation marks. Treat this information as indirect quotation.

Notes from fire station report:

> The local fire department received a call at 4:15 p.m. yesterday that a boy was stuck in the chimney of a house at 503 E. Vermont St.

> Firefighters used hammers and chisels to free the boy. They said the boy was so far down the chimney you couldn't see him from the roof. The boy told firemen he got home from school and found the house locked. He figured he could get in by crawling down the chimney like Santa Claus. He's a little guy. Only 8 years old.

> His mother came home about 4 o'clock and heard the boy screaming. When she figured out where he was, she called firefighters.

The boy's parents are Bill and Nancy Brown, who live at the above address with their three sons.

(The following information was obtained during telephone interviews. Direct quotes appear inside quote marks.)

Lt. Jim Stauss, a firefighter, said: "The boy looked like a little old chimney sweep when we got him out. He was scared, but he's a tough little guy. He will be all right. Good thing we've got a couple of bricklayers in the department. They told us how and where to cut and chisel to get him out. We started at the top of the chimney and worked down to his feet. He was upside down in the chimney. It took us about 30 minutes to get him out."

The boy's mother said: "His name is Andy. He's our youngest. He's all right. His only injury was a chipped tooth. He was screaming when I arrived, but I had a hard time locating him because he was stuck upside down in the chimney. I asked him why he tried to go down the chimney and he said he figured he could get in the house like Santa Claus. He's not sure he believes in Santa Claus after getting stuck in the chimney."

Assignment:

Write a short feature story based on the information that is now available to you. You will need to include most of the 5Ws and H in your feature, but you can organize the story as a feature article rather than as a news story. Save one of the direct quotes for use as your "kicker" to conclude the feature article. Double space your article and make certain that your name appears in the top left corner. Turn in the assignment and discuss it with your teacher.

Note to Teacher:

This incident qualifies as news. The first story is written as a simple inverted-pyramid news story in which the most important information is presented first. The student's assignment should illustrate how a news report can be featurized. The art of story-telling comes into play, and the writer delays telling what happens. This is made possible because the writer has a number of direct quotes and detailed information to work with.

A featurized lead might read:

No one was at home and the house was locked when Andy Brown showed up after school yesterday afternoon. So, he decided to crawl down the chimney like Santa Claus.

"He was screaming when I arrived," his mother said, "but I had a hard time locating him because he was stuck upside down in the chimney."

It took firefighters 30 minutes to cut away the bricks and to rescue Andy, son of Bill and Nancy Brown, at 503 E. Vermont St. His only injury was a chipped tooth…. [Details follow in chronological form]

The story ends with this kicker.

"I asked him why he tried to go down the chimney and he said he figured he could get in the house like Santa Claus," his mother said. "He's not sure he believes in Santa Claus after getting stuck in the chimney."

Writing a Hobby Article

Story ideas don't drop into a writer's lap. The writer acquires them by searching and by asking questions. For example, a news story might raise a question that is best answered in a feature article. Or the writer hears about a person who has recently had an interesting experience. Or the writer is assigned to write about someone who has an interesting hobby. In this case, the writer may know someone who builds kites and attempts to duplicate Ben Franklin's electrical experiments during thunderstorms, or someone who raises rabbits, races turtles, collects dolls or builds model airplanes.

So, the writer begins to ask questions, locates someone with an interesting hobby, makes an appointment for a face-to-face interview and does some background research on the hobby. The writer also may wish to take photographs that can be used to illustrate the feature article. As we will learn, photographs often help sell feature articles to editors of newspapers and magazines.

Assignment:

Interview a person outside your family about that person's hobby. Then write a 500-word article. Turn in your notes and the first draft of the article to your teacher. After the article is critiqued by your teacher, prepare a final draft for your permanent writing file.

Suggestions:

1. Locate a person outside your family who has an interesting hobby.

2. Phone that person, identify yourself and explain that you would like to write a story about their hobby. Make an appointment for a face-to-face interview. Tell the person you plan to write an article for publication. If the person says he/she doesn't want to be identified or quoted in the article, find someone else with an interesting hobby to interview.

3. You may wish to visit a library and to find out as much as you can about the hobby before you conduct the interview.

4. When you begin your face-to-face interview, explain again the purpose of the interview. Make it clear that you plan to identify the person by name and to quote that person in your story. If the person refuses to be identified or says, "I don't want this published," end the conversation quickly and seek out another respondent.

5. Take notes during the interview. As you complete the interview, ask permission to call that person if you have additional questions or wish to check information and quotes.

6. Then write a 500-word feature article about the person and his/her hobby. As part of the article you may wish to include some of the information you have researched about the hobby.

7. Follow the essay format in organizing your article but write short paragraphs. Remember to introduce the subject in an interesting manner and to make the point of your article clear to the reader.

8. If you type or write your article on a computer, double space. Your name and a short title for the article should appear on the first page of your manuscript. Example:

Sam's World of Wood

By (student's name)

The story begins a third of the way down the page. Indent paragraphs five spaces and double space the text of your story.

Hobby Story Examples:

The following introductions to hobby feature articles were written by ninth and tenth grade home school students:

The Indian carefully carves the cedar wood into a basket. She lines the inside of it with leaves, then walks to the berry patch.

The basket, knee-high with an upward arch in the bottom, hangs from her neck and rests on her knee. She is now free to use both hands to pick berries.

When the basket is full, she rides her horse to a small house. There she presents the basket of berries to the woman living there.

The woman, in turn, uses the basket to hold her umbrellas. Later, she passes it down to her niece, Edythe Wolfe, who still has it today.

Wolfe, 86, has collected baskets all her life. She now has 493 of them. Almost all were gifts. The Indian basket is her favorite.[12]

* * *

"N7NPA calling 3YOPI Peter II Island" crackled the small ham radio that occupies a corner of Scott Wood's living room. This moment on Feb. 2, 1994, was Wood's most exciting experience as a ham radio operator.

Although reaching the island off the coast of Antarctica was the most exciting experience, Woods says it was not the most interesting because the conversation was only an exchange of call letters.

---

12. Written by Krista Bernard, a home school student.

"The most interesting conversation was with a man who lived on the Island of Tonga in a grass hut." In very broken English this man told Wood about his family and the way they lived.

Wood, who lives near the small town of Crow on Wolf Creek Road, has been involved with the hobby since 1989.[13]

Note to Teacher:

The hobby assignment may require two or more weeks to complete, depending on how soon the student can arrange and conduct an interview.

Lesson 14 does not contain an assignment. It is written primarily for teachers although students may opt to read it. The lesson offers additional suggestions for organizing and writing the feature story and for critiquing a student's work.

---

13. Written by Holly Rogers, a home school student.

Jazzing Up the Story

Note to Teacher:

A beginning feature writer often has difficulty organizing the story. The first hurdle may be to create a focus statement on which to hang the rest of the story. That problem is one of the reasons the student was assigned to write about a hobby.

The focus of a hobby article usually is obvious and broad-ranging. For example, any biographical information normally helps introduce the hobbyist to the reader and may offer clues about why that person chose a particular hobby. The student who fails to gather biographical information should be encouraged to do so by talking again with the respondent either in person or by phone. The student may have other questions to ask or may need to check the accuracy of quotes and information gathered in the original interview.

The student also may need help organizing the introduction. Even though the student may have written personal and family history stories, essays and short stories, the task of selecting information to introduce a focus statement can be daunting. The student may have difficulty recognizing an incident, anecdote or scene-setter in his/her notes that will serve as an introduction.

After the method of introducing the article is determined, the writer should consider how best to tell the story. For example:

1. Avoid beginning the article with a question. Rules are made to be broken, but writers normally are expected to answer questions.
2. The time element usually is unimportant in a feature article. So, the writer can use present tense, active verbs throughout the story. Examples: Andy Brown recalls the day he nearly lost his camera. A dark-haired cook, dressed in jeans and a T-shirt, adds a little of this and a little of that...

The middle-section of a feature story often can be told in chronological order. For example: After the respondent's hobby is introduced, the story can trace how the person became interested in and developed the hobby. An occasional direct quote should be incorporated to give the story life and a sense of immediacy.

Chronology often will ensure smooth transition from sentence to sentence, paragraph to paragraph and thought to thought. Mechanical transitional words and phrases such as *therefore, moreover, however, on the other hand* may be needed.

Remember, too, that beginning students will often write short. In other words, they may have difficulty writing a hobby feature of 500 words. As they become more adept at interviewing and gathering information, they will often complain because "we don't have enough space" to tell the story. The problem then becomes a matter of selecting the best material to include in the story.

The teacher should serve as a friendly editor in the writing process by encouraging, challenging and correcting the student.

While every writer needs an editor, most writers resent suggestions and corrections. The writer is a creator, an artist, and will feel hurt and will become defensive when his/her "creation" has been questioned or fiddled with.

Keep in mind, too, that this may be one of the first writing projects a student has undertaken alone. The student locates a person with a hobby, interviews the respondent and writes a first draft. Now, the teacher/editor gets involved and begins to question the article's organization, choice of material, sentence structure, spelling, etc. Be prepared for opposition and even resentment.

By this time, however, the student should be accustomed to writing a first draft for critiquing by his/her teacher. Some of the pressure and resentment can be relieved if the teacher/editor verbally discusses the first draft, asking for explanations from the student. The teacher/editor can then offer suggestions about such things as story organization and selection of material. In any event, leave the final decisions to the student, who should be given a realistic deadline for completing a second draft.

Look for things to praise in the first draft. Point out areas of the student's writing that are improving. If the feature article looks promising, suggest ways that it might eventually be published. Maybe copies of the final draft could be circulated to the respondent and to members of the family. Maybe the article will be suitable for submission to a neighborhood newspaper.

The student is learning how to interview and how to use words to communicate important and interesting information to an audience. *The Write Stuff Adventure* may be an arduous and sometimes frightening experience, but it is a trip whose lessons will be remembered and used for a lifetime.

What's Cookin'?

A feature article about a cook or baker should be easy to research and write. Someone in the family is acquainted with a neighbor or a person who is known for his/her cooking or baking. Why that person is popular or well-known as a cook or baker can serve as the focus of the interview and story. Or why a recipe is the respondent's favorite. The respondent's history of cooking will be important to know. How and when the respondent prepares a favorite food dish is worth discovering. A favorite recipe is an added ingredient for this feature and concludes the article.

Most newspapers publish a food page, which may be a potential market for your story. Suggestions on how to market this feature appear in Lesson 18, "Marketing Your Mousetrap."

Assignment:

Find someone outside your family who enjoys cooking or baking. It should be a person who has developed a recipe or who is well known for cooking a particular dish or for baking a certain kind of pastry. Make this inquiry immediately, today. Your respondent may not be available for an interview on short notice. Meanwhile, prepare a focus statement and a list of questions to ask during an interview.

Arrange a face-to-face interview with the respondent. Find out something about how your respondent became interested in cooking or baking and how that person eventually developed and refined the recipe. Make it clear that you plan to offer the article and the recipe to a newspaper or magazine for publication.

Take notes during the interview. Maybe the respondent will prepare the recipe for you while you are conducting the interview. Obtain a written copy of the recipe from the respondent. Include the ingredients and how to prepare the recipe as part of your article. You may need some help in transcribing the recipe from a member of your family who cooks and bakes.

Plan to write at least 500 and not more than 750 words, plus the recipe, in an article for submission to the food page of your local newspaper. Make certain that your respondent understands that you plan to use his/her name and that you plan to submit the story for publication.

Double space the article. Turn in your notes with your article. After your teacher critiques the article, revise it and prepare a final draft for your permanent writing file.

Note to Teacher:

This is the second of three major features assigned during this unit of study and may require more than a week to complete. One article acquaints the student with gathering information through interviews and with organizing and writing a non-fiction article. The second article provides practice in developing these skills. The third article will test the student's ability to create a story idea and to develop it into an article suitable for publication in a newspaper, magazine, newsletter or some other medium.

A Word of Caution:

Writers, especially beginners, often procrastinate in arranging interviews. Insist that your student get cookin' on this project. If the student completes a final draft of this article in less than three weeks, take a short break or move to the next lesson.

Student Example:

The following feature article was written by Stephanie Rea, a home school eighth grader. It concludes with a recipe for Guava Sauce. The story was titled, "Cooking in Zaire."

Between meals in Zaire, Africa, the Hazen children grabbed a banana from the bunch hanging from the porch roof where they ripened. It was the common snack for the four growing children.

Guavas are another snack the children liked. The fruit is round or pear-like, 1 1/2 to 2 inches in diameter. They have peels like oranges, though they are eaten. Guavas have many small seeds that are easier to eat than to sort through.

Although these fruits were abundant, the Hazens had to live without many foods found in the United States. As a result, Ruth Hazen had to learn new tricks and many different ways to cook and bake in Zaire.

The last year that the Hazen family was in Zaire, Ruth had a real kitchen. The stove had three burners and an oven that worked. When the electricity went out, sometimes for three weeks, Ruth used a babula, a charcoal stove that was used outside. Ruth would make soup or stew in a large pot.

"We always kept it outside, right on the ground," she said. One year Ruth had a gas stove because the family didn't have electricity.

Before the Hazen family traveled to Zaire to be missionaries, Ruth became nervous. She didn't know what she was going to do without a convenient grocery store.

The "white man's stores" in Zaire were smaller than Dari Mart stores. They usually were owned by French or Indian people. Though food imported from Europe was expensive, Ruth bought the basics. She bought 50-pound sacks of flour and sugar and bags of powdered milk. She bought mustard powder, Blue Band, which is margarine, and salt.

Instead of buying some foods at the store, Ruth learned how to make them. She made mayonnaise and tomato sauce. With mustard powder she made mustard.

The Hazens had a garden the last year that they were there.

"We could grow our own lettuce, cucumbers, carrots, peanuts, green beans, potatoes, celery cabbage and rhubarb," Ruth said.

In some parts of the country the ground was too rocky for a garden. When the Hazens couldn't grow vegetables, they bought them at the market. Ruth said that people would see them coming. They would run to the car and shove produce through the windows.

"Everyone wanted your business," she said.

Ruth said that she had to learn how to bargain. She said that if she were bargaining with one person over something like tomatoes, another person selling that vegetable would come with a better price.

"I had to say, 'No, I am working with this person,'" Ruth said.

The Hazens had to learn to eat Zairian-grown vegetables. The peas were bigger and harder. Corn on the cob, green beans and onions also were different than American-grown vegetables.

Ruth purchased fresh meat from a butcher and had to learn new ways to cook and bake meat. She had to grind beef, and she sometimes made a gravy-meat dish. Ruth made jerky when she knew that the family was going on a trip. They also ate goat meat and chicken.

The Hazens raised chickens so that they wouldn't have to buy eggs.

"The chickens laid real well, and that was nice because eggs are expensive, about 40 to 50 cents apiece," Ruth said. She learned that egg souffle was an easy meal to make when she was in a hurry.

A man that was half Belgian and half African sold the Hazens cheese. It was close to a white mozzarella. Ruth put it in everything that called for cheese.

From a missionary cookbook Ruth got the recipe for making graham crackers. She learned how to make pasta with a pasta maker and she made granola.

Ruth found out all the ways that bananas can be used. She dried, fried and cooked them and made muffins and bread and banana cream pies.

The Hazen children loved picking and eating guavas, but there were always more guavas picked than eaten. The children's school teacher and Ruth made a recipe that would use the extra guavas by saucing them. The dish is called Guava Sauce. Ruth said that she made it every two weeks.

"It's like apple sauce," Ruth said. "Everyone liked it, so they ate it up fast."

Marketing the Mousetrap

You have heard stories about people who invent a better mousetrap. One that catches mice easily. One that doesn't hurt the mice it traps. One that is easy to set. One that is inexpensive. One that is long-lasting. A great mousetrap, you say, but how do I sell it?

The answer to that question is one sought by writers of feature articles. How do I get the article published? Who will buy it and for how much?

Don't wait. Seek that answer now. You could, of course, make several copies of your story and distribute them with members of your extended family and friends. Or you could interview several cooks and bakers in your neighborhood and publish a cookbook. But most writers don't want to be bothered with the expense and with the work of self-publishing.

In the previous lesson, the food section of your local newspaper was suggested as a market. Or maybe the newspaper publishes a teen page that accepts work of student writers. Don't overlook contests in home school and other publications. You also may be able to sell the article to a magazine that features recipes.

Assignment:

Decide on a market for your recipe article. Write what is called a cover letter to the editor of that publication. The letter should be no longer than one page, should be single spaced and should include your name, address and a summary of how you went about gathering the information and writing the article. Explain that you have permission from the respondent to publish the article and that the respondent is willing to have his/her picture taken to illustrate the article.

As soon as your teacher approves the final draft of your feature article, send a copy with your cover letter to the editor. Include a stamped envelope bearing your address so that the editor can respond to your submission. Authors refer to this letter as an SASE.

Don't expect an immediate response. An editor of a local newspaper may answer your letter in a week. An editor of a magazine may not respond for several weeks.

Don't despair if the editor returns your article with a printed rejection slip. Free-lance writers are accustomed to this type of response. Date and place rejection slips and letters of rejection from editors in your permanent writing file. Then find another market and submit your article and cover letter again.

Note to Teacher:

The cover letter can be short and to the point. The student should explain why the article was written and should include a short biographical statement of the student's grade, age, etc. Include a telephone number so the editor can contact the student.

A Sample Cover Letter:

1220 Clinton Drive
Eugene, OR 97401
Month, Day, Year

John Doe, Editor
The Food Section
Name of Newspaper
Street Address
City, State ZIP

Dear Mister Doe:

Your readers will want to know how to shake and bake "A Greaseless Doughnut" by reading the enclosed story that I wrote as a home school writing assignment.

I interviewed Jackie Bingham, who is famous for baking greaseless doughnuts at a local mom-and-pop cafe. The recipe is included in this story of 600 words. Jackie has given permission for this story to be published, and she is willing to be photographed.

I am an eighth grader who is home schooled by my mother and father. I am interested in becoming a classical pianist. I am also a member of the 4-H Rapid Rabbit Club and participate in my church's youth group. I am a member of the South High School swim team and like to fly my dad's airplane in my spare time.

If you decide to print this story, please use my middle name as well as my first and last in the byline. If you have questions, you can call me or leave a message at (000) 000-000.

Sincerely,

Dan Deano Rea

Greetings

Roses are red
Violets are blue
Cards need verses
Written by you.

Americans purchase about a half million greeting cards annually, according to the Greeting Card Association. They account for about 50 percent of all first-class mail. As a result, greeting card companies, large and small, flourish. To stay in business they need a constant supply of messages and illustrations to print on those cards. Some companies employ writers to create these messages. Others buy poetry, rhymes, messages and ideas for illustrations from free-lancers.

These companies pay for this material, which often is incentive enough to stir up the creative juices of any writer who has the ability to "turn a phrase," be humorous and/or serious.

The best and most current guide for how to write for the greeting card and gift idea market is the *Writer's Digest.* This resource is published annually by Writer's Digest Books and should be in the reference section of a public library. A chapter normally is devoted to describing this market and how to write for it. A list of publishers and their requirements are included.

Assignment:

Find a market in *Writer's Digest* or select a local greeting card company that may not be listed in this market guide. Learn the manuscript submission guidelines for that publisher and submit several messages suitable for a greeting card. Note that some publishers want seasonal material several months in advance. Some will list word limits and others will suggest the number of ideas that may be submitted. Some want each submission written on a 3- by 5-inch card. Others want these messages written on 8 1/2- by 11-inch paper.

Don't forget to include a short cover letter and an SASE when you submit your greeting card messages or gift ideas. And don't expect a reply for several months.

The general practice is to submit free-lance articles and other material to only one publisher at a time. Of course, if one publisher rejects your greeting card messages, you are free to send them to another publisher.

Note to Teacher:

Encourage the student to browse through a greeting card section of a local store and note what kind of messages appear on cards. (This might be a good time to discuss plagiarism with your student.) Some greeting card companies may want ideas for illustrations to accompany messages.

If you know of a local greeting card company, it may be worthwhile to talk with a representative. Find out how to submit material to that market. Most established publishers will return free guidelines to writers who request them and include an SASE.

Like all free-lance writing, the greeting card market is one that can be pursued for a lifetime. Many people from all walks of life write and submit material to publishers while caring for a family or while working at some other job.

Field Trip:

This might be a good time to arrange a visit with a free-lance writer in your community. Most free-lancers are willing to describe how they became interested in writing and how they pursue that interest. Most are teachers at heart and are willing to share how-to tips on gathering information, interviewing and writing. Make it a threesome of you, the student and the free-lance writer.

Writing for Publication

We have been learning the craft and perfecting the art of writing a non-fiction feature article. It is time that we put these skills to work by writing for publication.

Granted, you have written articles and greeting card messages suitable for publication as practice projects. Now, the full responsibility for selecting a story idea and for developing it into a salable article falls on the shoulders of you, the student.

As you know, two things are essential if a feature article is to be sold and they often are of equal importance: 1) the story idea and 2) the market. Therefore, as the writer considers various story ideas, the question of who would buy and/or publish the feature article is equally important.

The simplest approach is to write a feature for a church newsletter or for some specialized publication in your community that uses volunteer writers. Articles in these publications often focus on an individual or upon a program.

The editor may have suggestions, even assignments, available for free-lance writers. The payment may be no more than a byline and publication of the article, but that often is pay enough for a beginning writer. A copy of a published article is a "clip" that can be placed in the writer's permanent writing file.

Other opportunities abound, but you should study markets, including youth magazines and general circulation newspapers, especially those with feature sections.

Assignment:

Pick a market to match your story idea, gather material through research and at least one interview, write a non-fiction feature article and submit it to that market. Include a cover letter and an SASE with a copy of your double-spaced article.

Discuss your idea for a feature article and market with your teacher and invite your teacher to critique your first draft. Match the length of the article to the requirements of your market. Some markets may want an article of 500 words. Others may want as many as 3,000 words. Keep your audience of readers in mind as you research and write this article. If at first you don't succeed, send the article to a second publisher. Some revising may be needed to meet the specialized needs of the second publisher.

This assignment should be completed in less than a month's time and concludes your formal study of non-fiction article writing. Place a copy of this assignment in your permanent writing file.

Note to Teacher:

A student's interest in writing may be flagging this late in the school year. This project, however, offers a realistic look at free-lance writing as a part-time or full-time career. It's tough work and the effort often is unrewarded by publication and by income. For those of us who want to write—must write—the adventure results in a lifetime filled with working with wonderful words.

Section Five:

News, Advertising and Photography

Note to Teacher

The writing craft continues to be explored in this fifth unit of *The Write Stuff Adventure*. It opens with a look at how information is gathered and shared through the media, including newspapers and broadcast stations. The student will be introduced to the world of public relations, advertising and photography with a few unexpected stops along the journey.

The non-fiction news report is the basis of most information sharing in today's world. The vehicle may be a simple conversation with a friend or a news story. The writing and organizational tools that have been acquired and sharpened during earlier *Write Stuff* lessons will be helpful in writing a summary lead and in organizing the inverted pyramid news story. These lessons will lead to the publication of a family newspaper.

The "Write It Tight" section illustrates the need to tailor messages in such areas as advertising and broadcasting. Crossword puzzles, cartooning and cutlines are other areas worthy of exploration.

The final section, visual communication, often is the most popular among students who have spent several years working with words. Students are introduced to principles of visual composition and are encouraged to take photographs that will enhance their personal and family albums. Students often use point-and-shoot cameras and commercial outlets for developing and printing film.

Photography offers an excellent opportunity for a home school study group to teach photography, to pool resources and to present the work of students in an exhibit. If an art gallery or some other facility is used for the exhibit, those arrangements should be made as far in advance as possible, as is noted in Lesson 8 of the photo segment.

In a group show, photo enlargements of each student's three favorite negatives are recommended. An exhibit often runs for several weeks. Launch it with a reception, which creates an appropriate setting for public recognition of students who have participated in *The Write Stuff Adventure*.

News in Review

Lesson 1

The Topsy-turvy Essay

Our attention turns from essays and non-fiction articles to news stories. During this study, we will become acquainted with the inverted pyramid. We will learn how to identify news. We will write news stories, prepare a news release and publish a family newspaper.

Our first task is to turn the introduction of an essay upside down and to begin a news story with the thesis statement. This summarization of the essential information is referred to as the "lead" of a news story.

Journalists call this method of organizing a news story an "inverted pyramid." The story-teller reveals "who done it" immediately and then presents the details in a descending order of importance.

The switch in story organization should be relatively easy for anyone who has learned how to structure an essay. The inverted pyramid, however, often is difficult for the beginner because information may be repeated in a story.

Again, the student who has learned to focus an essay or a non-fiction article with a summary statement should be able to make the switch to news writing. For example: An essay or feature article might introduce a traffic accident by describing the scene before explaining that one of the drivers was critically injured. An inverted pyramid news story would lead with the injury.

Assignment:

Read the national and international sections of a daily newspaper for several days. Circle five stories that introduce all or most of the 5Ws and H (who, when, where, why, what and how) in the first paragraph or two. After the important news elements are introduced, the details will be presented. This section of the inverted pyramid is referred to as "elaboration." Discuss these stories with your teacher and then repeat the assignment later in the week.

Note that the traditional inverted pyramid can be "cut from the bottom," which means that an editor can shorten a story by deleting paragraphs starting from the bottom. Ideally, all but the first paragraph could be "cut" and a short news story would remain.

Because the inverted pyramid offers a short summary of the story in the lead, readers can skim the news by reading the headline and first paragraph of a story.

The inverted pyramid also facilitates rewriting of news stories to incorporate new information as it is received. Example: The driver of the car involved in an accident that occurred in front of your home was critically injured. In the first draft of a news story, the reporter writes this lead:

> A 27-year-old university student was critically injured this morning in a one-car accident on West 21st Avenue.

As the deadline approaches for publishing this story in a daily newspaper the reporter learns that the driver of the car has died. The lead can be updated by changing one word:

> A 27-year-old university student was *fatally* injured this morning in a one-car accident on West 21st Avenue.

Note to Teacher:

Not all 5Ws and the H will appear in the first paragraph, called the lead, in all inverted pyramid news stories. The lesser-important of the 5Ws and H may be summarized in the second paragraph, called the "catch-all." Note, too, that the "how" may not be reported because it is unknown or unavailable.

The trend today is to featurize news stories. For this reason, the student has been assigned to read the national and international news sections of a daily newspaper. These stories more often are structured as inverted pyramids to facilitate revision.

You can introduce your student to bylines, which are names of reporters that usually appear between a headline and the start of the story. Cities that appear in ALL CAPS at the beginning of a story are referred to as datelines, which designate the place where the story originated. Datelines are not used with local stories. The logotype (AP) refers to The Associated Press and (UPI) refers to the United Press International, news services whose dispatches may appear in a newspaper. These logotypes often will appear along with the dateline at the beginning of a story.

So, What Happened?

News has been defined as anything that interests a number of readers, viewers or listeners. The problem, however, is that so much information is available to the public today that journalists must be selective in what to write and to publish or broadcast.

They become what is known as "gatekeepers," people who discard and select information along the news chain leading to publication or broadcast. For example, a reporter may have enough information to write a 500-word story but is told by an editor to write a story half that long. The broadcast reporter may have to pare down a story to a "sound bite" of a few words.

Audience is also a factor in determining what is news. A community weekly that circulates in your neighborhood might report the auto accident that occurred in front of your home in detail. A metropolitan daily newspaper might not publish the story unless the driver of the car was killed.

We know, however, that local events often are more newsworthy to us than those that occur in other communities—that is, unless those events are filled with conflict or result in a number of deaths or widespread damage. Timeliness plays a role, too, because members of the media—newspapers, radio and television stations—are looking for the "latest angle" to share with readers, viewers and listeners. Nothing is as old as yesterday's news.

Once a decision is made that a particular event or incident is newsworthy, the reporter must gather information, which we have classified as the 5Ws and H.

What happened? When did it happen? Where did it happen? How and why did it happen? Who was involved? This research, which is called news-gathering, may be frustrated by news sources who are unavailable for comment, who cannot be located or who refuse to comment. Public records may be incomplete or unavailable to the reporter who is working "against the pressure of a deadline," which means the time you have to turn in a story to an editor.

Let's assume that the reporter has most of the basic information and enough details to write a story. How does he/she introduce the story? The answer, of course, is with the focus statement, which essay writers refer to as the thesis statement. For a reporter, the answer often is: What happened?

This question will force the reporter to summarize the point of the story so that this information is presented first in an inverted pyramid news story. This introduction is called a "lead." A summary of other essential information taken from the 5Ws and H either completes the lead or appears in the second paragraph referred to as the "catch-all."

Keep in mind that paragraphs are limited to one or two sentences in a news story in the same way as in a feature article. If your paragraph grows beyond four or five typewritten or computer-generated lines, look for ways to shorten it or begin a new paragraph.

First Assignment:

Study the first two paragraphs of five news stories that appear in the national and international sections of a daily newspaper. Identify as many of the 5Ws and H as possible in each of the stories. Then discuss the focus statement in each story with your teacher. Ideally, an inverted pyramid story will introduce the most important or significant information in the first sentence.

Example: Two people died in an accident at the Sixth Street railroad crossing early this morning.

Second Assignment:

Write a news story based on some recent incident involving a member of your family.

Examples: The family cat gave birth yesterday to a litter of five kittens. A brother fell while playing in a tree and suffered a fractured arm.

After introducing the incident in the lead of your story, elaborate by reporting details of the incident.

Write the story in the third person, which means that you cannot be the source of information. In other words, you are not to include first-person references of *I, me, my* in the story. Use first and last names when a person is introduced in the story. You cannot refer to someone as "my sister" or "my father."

Your name and the date the story was written should appear at the top of your story, which should be double spaced. Turn in the story to your teacher, who will critique your work and may require a revision. Place a copy of the final draft in your permanent writing file.

Note to Teacher:

The first assignment is designed to introduce the student to news values. Conflict often is involved in determining whether something is newsworthy. Other guidelines include significance of the event, the importance of a person, whether the event is of interest to a local audience, curiosity and timeliness. Significance may be measured, for example, by the number of people involved or affected by an incident or by some action of a public official or body.

The second assignment gives the student a chance to determine what he/she considers to be newsworthy and then to share that information by writing a news story. Encourage the student to write a story of at least two paragraphs, one that summarizes the information and one that contains details. If the student has overlooked any information, suggest that it be incorporated in a second draft.

For those students who show a particular interest in news writing, suggest that they write a second story.

Example of a news story written by Calvin Doe:

Five kittens were born yesterday to Jessica, a cat that makes her home with the John Doe family.

The kittens already have been named by the children, Wendy, 6, and by Calvin, 12. The names are Donner, Blitzen, Jasmine, Snow White and Snoopy.

"I like Jasmine the best," Wendy said. "She's so nice and soft and I want to keep her."

Jessica was a stray Tabby cat that the Doe family decided to keep when she showed up on the doorstep a year ago. She sleeps in the basement but is let outdoors every morning.

The Doe family has two other pets, a dog named Skip and a rooster named Crow. The family lives at 1220 Clayton Street.

Quotes and Attribution

The reporter, like the feature article writer, must rely primarily on information gleaned from other sources. While it is important for a reporter to be able to describe something that he/she observes, most information is gathered from and attributed to other sources. A reporter is just that: a reporter. The reporter is not to express a personal point of view in a news story. Rather, the reporter mirrors the news by reporting information collected through research and by interviewing people in person or by telephone. Therefore, it is important to know how to handle quotes and attribution.

Before continuing, review the quotes and notes sections in Lesson 2 of Section 4: Interviewing and the Non-Fiction Article. Direct quotes should be the verbatim comments of a person. They appear inside double quote marks. A writer often wishes to rearrange or to shorten a statement. To do this, the quote marks should be deleted. In most cases, a writer may paraphrase or use his/her own words to summarize something attributed to a source.

As a reminder, here are examples of how direct quote and paraphrase would be written and attributed to a source:

"I will vote in favor of the bill to reduce taxes," Mayor John Doe said. (The direct quote is attributed to the mayor. The source is set off or separated from the quote by a comma.)

Mayor John Doe said he will vote to reduce taxes. (The mayor's remark has been paraphrased by the writer.)

Assignment:

Identify five direct quotes and five paraphrased statements that appear in stories published by a daily newspaper. Each of them should be attributed to a source. Discuss these quotes and statements with your teacher and note how they are punctuated. Then write a news story about some incident that occurred recently in your family or neighborhood. Attribute each statement that appears in the story to a source except the summary statement in your lead. Interview at least one person who was involved in the incident and include one or more direct quotes in the story. Discuss the story with your teacher and rewrite it. Place a final draft in your permanent writing file.

Story Example:

Three pigs destroyed a garden after breaking out of their pen yesterday at the John Doe farm.

"The pigs broke through a wooden fence late in the afternoon," John Doe said, "and ended up in our garden nearby."

"They rooted up all of the vegetables and knocked over my tomato plants," Jane Doe said. "I guess I'll not be canning much this year."

The pigs are family pets, she explained. They were purchased last spring and were being raised to show at the county fair, she added.

"I've fixed the fence and those pigs won't get out again," he said.

Note to Teacher:

The normal practice is to use "said" in attribution rather than such substitutes as "exclaimed," "pointed out," "proclaimed." Reporters normally follow the subject/verb order in writing attribution: "Doe said" rather than "said Doe." The exception to this guideline occurs when an appositive or dependent clause follows the name: said Doe, president of Acme Asphalt Service. Examples of correct usage: The well ran dry, Doe said. The well ran dry, said Doe, president of Acme Asphalt Service. (Note that neither of the examples is a direct quote. Any person, including a teacher, who edits a story should not add direct quote marks to a story without first consulting the writer. The statement attributed to a quote may have been changed or paraphrased by the writer. Fabrication of direct quotes not only is dishonest, but also will destroy trust that a source may have in a reporter.)

Simple Stories

The simple news story normally involves an uncomplicated incident or topic and often is based on information provided by a single source. The next step in *The Write Stuff Adventure* will be to practice writing three of these stories.

Assignment:

Write separate stories on separate sheets of paper based on the information provided below. Turn in your stories to the teacher, who will critique and return them to you for revision.

The top three lines of your first page should contain the following information, which should be single spaced and appear in the top left corner:

Your first and last name
A brief story summary
The date the story was written

Drop down a few lines and begin your double-spaced story.

House Fire

The fire department responded to an alarm at 11 p.m. yesterday. Two fire trucks were dispatched to the home of Tom and Cecelia Jackson at 2145 South Hemlock Street.

Firefighters found the two-story frame building engulfed in flames. The Jacksons and their two children escaped from the building. They were putting their girls to bed when they smelled smoke and saw it coming from the attic. He and his wife carried their twin daughters from an upstairs bedroom and called the fire department. The girls are 1 year old and their names are Jessie and Jasmine.

Firefighters extinguished the blaze in 15 minutes but damage to the upstairs bedrooms was extensive. Damage was estimated at $25,000. The family said it had insurance to cover the damage to the building and to the contents.

Lost Dog

The mayor was late for the City Council meeting last night. He said later that he had been searching for the family dog, Lassie.

"Lassie escaped through a gate that someone left open at home," Mayor Bill Morse explained today. "We have looked everywhere in the neighborhood without success." The Morse family lives at 21340 Blueberry Hill.

The mayor said he received a call from his daughter, Nellie, who discovered Lassie missing when she arrived home from school yesterday. The mayor joined her and several neighbors in an unsuccessful search of the neighborhood. That made him 15 minutes late for the council meeting.

Early this morning, however, the mayor reported that Lassie had been found. "She showed up at home about 7 a.m.," he said. "We don't know where she has been, and she wasn't hungry. Someone must have taken her in for the night and fed her."

Lassie is a 4-year-old Collie who has been raised by the Morse family since she was a puppy.

"That's the first time that she's been away from home," the mayor said. "I hope no one will leave the gate open again."

Neighborhood Party

Plans have been announced for a special event to take place at the Eastside Community Center.

The event will take place next Saturday from 1 p.m. to 4 p.m. East Side neighborhood residents are invited. No admission will be charged.

The event has been titled "Partytime." It is an annual event and this will be the fifth year that it has been conducted.

Games for children and adults are planned throughout the afternoon. Games will include a three-legged race, free throw shooting, a 40-yard dash and building sand castles. Ribbons and prizes are being sponsored by the National Bank. Refreshments are being contributed by the Downtown Grocery Store.

People interested in attending should park their vehicles in the community center's lot at 10th and Oak Streets.

The Downtown Ragtime Band and the Sixth Regiment Drum and Bugle Corps will provide entertainment.

Note to Teacher:

The story summary mentioned in the three single-spaced lines that are to appear at the top left of the page is referred to as the slug line or slug. This is a one- to three-word summary that quickly identifies the story as it moves through the editing process. Note that slug lines have been provided for the three assigned stories.

You may want to check the student's first story before he/she continues with the second.

You will notice, for example, that the lead of the story does not appear first in the notes above. The lead has been buried. Therefore, it is important for the student to select the most newsworthy element and to place it in the first sentence of the news story.

Several different leads to the house fire story could be written. Two examples: A local couple escaped from a house fire last night with their 1-year-old twins; A fire caused an estimated $25,000 damage to a residence last night.

The dog has been found in the second story. Granted, the writer could "back into" this story by beginning with the mayor being late for the City Council meeting. But Lassie returned home and everyone should be happy. Keep in mind that prominence is an important news criterion. The mayor is the top city official and is more newsworthy than many other residents.

The neighborhood party sounds like a lot of fun. The lead should pick up some of this anticipated excitement and "catch" the reader's eye. Eastside residents probably are aware of the event but will appreciate the reminder and especially details about the time, place and nature of the event. A properly drafted news release would be of more help to a newspaper or broadcast station interested in publicizing the neighborhood party. In Lesson 8, we will learn how to prepare such a news release.

A Family Newspaper

Writing, editing and publishing a family newspaper can illustrate the importance of news. It also can be an enjoyable project that will command the interest of family members.

A name is needed for your newspaper. Incorporate the family name in titles like The Johnson Journal, The Quigley Times, The Franklin Herald. The newspaper could look like the one published in your community, but that would require a desktop publishing program and more effort than needed for this project.

Follow the example that appears at the end of this lesson. It will fit any 8 1/2- by 11-inch format and can be typed, computer-generated or written out in longhand. Notice that a major story tops the list and several short stories follow.

Assignment:

1. Pick a name for your newspaper.

2. Write an inverted pyramid news story about a major event involving a member of your family that has occurred during the past week. The story should be at least five paragraphs long.

3. Write six other inverted pyramid news stories about members of your family. Each story should be one- to two-paragraphs long.

4. You can write news stories about yourself but you cannot use first or second person. Substitute your name for personal pronouns.

5. After your teacher critiques your stories, make corrections and revisions. These stories will be used when you write headlines and complete the family newspaper in Lesson 6.

Note to Teacher:

Make certain that the student writes inverted pyramid news stories. Many of them may be of interest only to members of the family, which is fine because that is the student's audience.

The student may encounter difficulty in reporting events in which he/she is involved. You may have to illustrate how to substitute a name for a personal pronoun. Example:

(Wrong) I won the 100-meter dash in the city's All-Comer's Meet yesterday.

(Right) John Doe won the 100-meter dash in the city's All-Comer's Meet yesterday.

(Wrong) My brother sang "All's Well That Ends Well" during the Downtown Club's talent show last week. He didn't win but had lots of fun.

(Right) Phil Doe sang "All's Well That Ends Well" but failed to win in the Downtown Club's talent show last week.

Family Newspaper Example:

Names of family members appear in **boldface** in the following example to illustrate how to avoid the use of personal pronouns. Note, too, that ages appear as figures and are used as appositives. First names are used on second reference. A journalist, however, would use the last name on second reference. Today, the practice is to use a woman's first name rather than the Mrs., Miss or Ms. title. Rather than refer to Mr. and Mrs. John Doe, the writer would use the woman's name: John and Sally Doe.

The Family Herald

Publication Date   Phil Doe, editor   1234 Hillside Drive

Family Visits County Fair

Sally Doe won a 6-foot-tall teddy bear by knocking down three bottles with a baseball at the Dade County Fair last Thursday. Her husband and three children cheered after she won the prize, which she added to her collection.

"I knew she would knock down the bottles," her **husband Jack** said. "She was a great softball player in high school and can throw with the best of them."

"I now have 73 teddy bears that I began collecting when I was 10 years old," **Sally** said. "I won't tell you how many years ago that was," she added with a laugh.

Other members of the family failed to hit the bottles when they threw but enjoyed the rides, the exhibits and the food, especially the corn-on-the-cob and fried chicken.

Phil Doe, 12, won a red ribbon for a photograph he entered in the fair. It was a picture of his grandparents, **Joe and Jessica Franklin**, that he took on their 55th wedding anniversary. It shows them playing marbles on their hands and knees like they did when they were growing up together on neighboring farms in Ohio.

"My favorite ride was the ferris wheel," said **Amy Doe**, 6. "I wanted to go on the death-dodger thing-a-ma-jig, but my mother wouldn't let me."

Nate Begins Piano Lessons

Nate Doe, 9, started taking piano lessons Saturday from Dolly Smith, who also taught his **mother Sally** when she was a girl. **Nate** has been taking lessons from his mother. He also plays the trumpet, sax and drums. His teacher told him his first recital probably would be in six months. Dolly has 18 students.

10 Attend Slumber Party

Ten girls attended the 6th birthday party for Alice Hansen, including Amy Doe. They have been best friends for three years. After games were played and refreshments were served, gifts were opened. Amy said they stayed awake all night, laughing and telling stories.

Bike Repaired

After a flat tire was fixed, Phil Doe, 12, was able to ride his bike to the corner grocery to pick up a quart of pickles for his mother last week.

On the way home, however, Phil dropped and broke the jar of pickles. So, back to the store he went.

"I hit a bump and the sack just slipped from my hand," he said later.

Writing Headlines

Many newspaper readers scan headlines and consider that they have "read the paper" for the day. They can do this because most headlines are super-short summaries of a story's content. The news headline traditionally has been a mini-version of the inverted pyramid lead.

Try this experiment the next time you pick up a newspaper. Read only the headlines. In most cases, you may have no interest in reading farther. Even in those cases where some item catches your eye, your interest will wane after reading the first paragraph or two of the story. For example: A headline reads: Boy, 7, critical after accident. Your eye scans the story and you learn the boy's identity in the second paragraph. You don't know the boy or his family. Another headline on the page catches your eye and you move on. In less than five minutes you feel as though you are acquainted with the "news for the day."

Much the same happens with 5-minute news summaries that are broadcast during the day. If you listen to radio news updates, you feel informed about the world around you. Even telecast news shows essentially are news summaries.

In any event, news and feature stories require headlines, which are written by journalists known as copy editors. Traditionally, these editors check stories for errors in much the same way a teacher critiques a student's work. Stories are assigned to appear on certain pages and headlines are written.

Copy editors follow basic rules in writing headlines. Among those that we need to use are the following:

1. Be sure your headlines contain a subject and predicate and are in present tense, even though the incident or event has passed. Examples: Student wins award. Three receive gifts. Students doll up business district. Legislature passes bill.

2. Use "to" in signifying future tense. Examples: City to award contract. Legislature to consider tax proposal.

3. Omit articles—a, an, the—from headlines.

Assignment:

Write a one-line headline for each of the stories that you have prepared for your family newspaper. Follow the three guidelines that appear above.

After your teacher critiques the headlines, make corrections or rewrite. Then, create the final copy of your newspaper following the example that appears at the conclusion of Lesson 5. If you have a desktop publishing program, you may wish to create your own layout. In that case, the template may call for headlines of different sizes. If a headline is more than one line long, try to fill each line and avoid breaking up phrases between lines.

Example:
> Family wins award
> for largest pumpkin

When you have completed your newspaper and have received permission from your teacher, make enough copies to share with members of your extended family and friends. Don't forget to place a copy in your permanent writing file.

Note to Teacher:

This project should be an enjoyable one for the student. Information sources are close at hand, and the creative aspects of the project should enhance motivation to complete the assignment.

Remind the student that a newspaper or newsletter format can serve as a means of keeping family members informed after children are grown and begin rearing their own families. For example, a once-a-month summary of "what's happening in my life and in the life of my family" could be mailed, even e-mailed, much like a Christmas letter.

In any event, make certain that your student's newspaper is published and circulated.

The Reporter's Trade

When Ben Franklin began writing news stories in longhand in the early 1700s, type was set by hand, one letter at a time. Today, type is set as the writer composes a story on a computer. While technological change has revolutionized the printing craft during the past three centuries, the role of the storyteller remains unchanged. Today, storytellers who gather information and write it for publication or broadcast by the news media are called reporters.

You probably have learned that the media, or press, serve in an unofficial "watchdog role" in overseeing the three branches of government: executive, legislative and judicial. The media often are referred to as "the fourth branch of government," meaning that journalists are responsible for keeping citizens informed about how officials are conducting public affairs. This responsibility includes federal, state and local government.

Most citizens are unable to keep track of what their public officials are doing by attending meetings and discussing public affairs with officials. So, reporters serve as the eyes and ears of citizens by attending meetings of public agencies and by asking questions about the conduct of government. For example, a question often raised by a reporter is: Where is the money coming from and how is it being spent?

Reporters normally acquire the craft as they learn to gather information and write essays and articles in school. Daily newspapers usually require that a reporter be a college graduate. The reporter may be assigned to "cover" or be responsible for gathering information and writing stories on a "beat." Examples include the education beat, the police-fire beat and the local government beat.

As a newspaper employee, the reporter would work a certain schedule, which may require attending night meetings and writing stories "against a deadline." This means that the reporter must complete a story by a certain time. Presses must begin printing the paper at a precise time. Broadcasts cannot be delayed. As a result, the reporter masters the inverted pyramid form of organizing news and learns how to take notes rapidly, to organize news stories in his/her mind and to write quickly.

While the thought of conducting interviews with strangers and writing against deadline may frighten many beginners, the life of a reporter appeals to writers who like to meet people and to share what they learn. The desire to serve the public interest personified by Ben Franklin also continues to motivate men and women to be reporters nearly three centuries later.

Assignment:

Interview a reporter and write a story about his/her career based on the interview. Include some biography, direct quotes, etc. Introduce one version of the story with an inverted pyramid news lead and a second version with a feature lead. You may wish to add a "kicker" to the feature version.

From your previous study, you are aware that the reporter should be informed about the purpose of the interview when you call for an appointment and when you begin the interview.

Send copies of your stories to the reporter and place copies of the final draft in your permanent writing file.

Note to Teacher:

The student should be encouraged to schedule the time and place of an interview with a newspaper reporter. Ideally, the student should speak with the reporter on the job so that the student can become better acquainted with a newsroom. If possible, the interview should be face-to-face and a third party should not be present.

Remember, the focus statement should lead the inverted pyramid but should appear later in the featurized version. The student may wish to review Lesson 6 in Section Four: Interviewing and the Non-Fiction Article, which deals with story organization and the "kicker."

The News Release

Public relations is a career field whose popularity continues to grow. People who work in this field often represent companies, non-profit organizations and individuals who are offering goods, services and proposals to the public. A company may have a public relations representative or department. Others hire someone to handle a wide range of responsibilities, which include promoting the company, individual or product through news releases, public appearances, advertising and sponsorships.

Non-profit organizations often cannot afford to hire someone to publicize and to promote an event. They may have to call on volunteers, preferably those who know how to write. For this reason, a writer should be acquainted with how to construct a news release. In its simplest form, information is organized as an inverted-pyramid news story and contains the source's name, telephone number and a short headline.

Assignment:

You have been selected to write a news release about a home school play for distribution to three local newspapers, four radio stations, two television stations and several community fine arts groups.

The director of the play hands you written notes, which appear below. You are to assemble them into a news release, which should include your name and telephone number as the person to contact to answer questions. This information should appear at the top left of an 8 1/2- by 11-inch sheet of paper. Add a short one-line headline and then double space the news release. Include details about time, place and admission in a news release about a future event.

Turn in your news release for critiquing by your teacher. Make corrections and revisions. Then prepare a final draft. Include a copy in your permanent writing file.

News Release Notes:

(You may attribute this information to the director of the play, Hope Hannibal. Direct quotes appear inside double quote marks in the notes below. You are not at liberty to fabricate direct quotes.)

Event: a one-act play, "The Mysterious Stranger"
When: (two weeks from today, include month and day)
Time: 7 p.m.

Place: The Westside Community Church at 10255 East Main St.
Admission: Free
Sponsor: The Friday Home School Writing Group
Director: Hope Hannibal

Description of the play:

"The Mysterious Stranger" is the story of Dick and Jane, a brother and sister, who are constantly bickering but who decide to join forces when a stranger shows up at their home one afternoon while they are alone working on their home school assignments. The play was written by two 15-year-old home schoolers, Jack Jeffries and Marsha Franks. Four other students in the Friday Home School Writing Group appear in the play, which is being staged in the auditorium of the Westside Community Church. The other students are Abby Clements, Penny Anderson, Bob Black and Chester Everready.

 Comments by the director:

"I am extremely pleased with this talented group of home school students. Jack and Marsha volunteered to write the script and have been practicing faithfully with the other four students. I am certain that everyone will enjoy the performance."

"Parents have been supportive by building the set and by handling other administrative details."

Other information:

Jack Jeffries also plays trumpet in the Home School Symphonic Band. Last year Marsha Franks won the long jump competition in the city's All-Comer's Track and Field Meet. Both are members of their church youth groups.

Note to Teacher:

The news release should be organized as an inverted pyramid news story.

Broadcast stations probably will shorten the news release and major metropolitan newspapers also may rewrite and shorten the release.

Remember, the student should be required to rewrite the first draft after it has been critiqued.

Sell a Bike

Fifth and sixth grade students in *The Write Stuff Adventure* often found it difficult to fill a 100-word assignment.

"Can we write 80 words?" they would ask.

"How about 90?"

"Well, I don't have anything else to say."

This conversation changes several years later as students developed their information-gathering and writing skills.

"I can't write a 3,000-word short story."

"Why not?"

"I've already written 4,000 words, and I'm not done."

In the following series of lessons, brevity will be the watchword, the focus of the study.

People who write classified advertisements practice the art of brevity. They are super-summarizers of information. They write without the help of verbs and the articles, a, an and the. They capitalize the first word of the advertisement, which acts as a mini-headline.

Turn to the classified advertising section of a newspaper. Note that ads are placed under such headings as homes for sale, apartments for rent, appliances, household goods, help wanted and yard sales.

This type of advertising is valuable because the advertiser knows that people interested in these goods and services will be searching for this information. Classifieds also are less expensive than "display" ads published by businesses like department and grocery stores. A classified ad may cost several cents a word in a community weekly newspaper or several dollars a word in a metropolitan daily. Therefore, cost is important and the reason why classified ads contain abbreviations and omit words.

Assignment:

✓ Read classified ads under several headings and write a list of guidelines that you might follow in writing an ad.

✓ Then write a 15-word classified ad in which you offer your bicycle or some item you own for sale.

✓ Then write a 25-word classified ad in which you advertise all of your family's household items for sale.

✓ After your teacher has evaluated your work, make corrections and place the two ads in your permanent writing file.

Note to Teacher:

In discussing this topic with the student, explain that most newspapers have staff members who will assist in writing a want ad.

A check-list for use in your critique of the student's work:

✓ Many ads begin with a one- or two-word mini-headline which is CAPITALIZED.
✓ Abbreviations are used.
✓ Verbs and articles (a, an and the) may be omitted. Sentences often are incomplete.
✓ A telephone number is included.
✓ The price may be important.

Additional Note:

If your family has an item that could be sold, assign the student to write the ad and to make the sale. A commission may serve as an incentive and should prove educational.

Display the Message

Several types of advertising other than classified appear each day on the television screen, on the airwaves, in newspapers, magazines and other publications. These messages attempt to persuade the reader, viewer or listener to take some action: buy, sell, change a viewpoint. Millions of dollars are invested in marketing studies and in tailoring messages to audiences. Companies establish their own marketing and advertising departments or work with advertising and public relations agencies to promote products and the company image. Media experts also are prepared to create advertisements.

In *The Write Stuff Adventure*, however, we're taking a less expensive road. We're going to create our own advertisement that appears on a one-page flier or handout that can be posted in prime locations throughout the community.

Before we begin, however, we need to ask: What do we want to say? What is our focus? What is our thesis statement? After that question has been answered, we can decide the best selling points, whether we need an illustration and what to include in a headline and copy block, which is the text or elaboration section.

Assignment:

Because you're a writer, the Friday Home School Group asks you to publicize the annual "Get Acquainted With Home School Fair" in your community. You have been given permission to design and print 100 circulars that are 8 1/2 by 11 inches.

You can use any of the following information in designing the flier:

This is the 10th annual Get Acquainted With Home School Fair sponsored by the county home school association. The theme of the fair is "The Internet as a Textbook." The date is the first Saturday in the next month, based on the time this assignment is undertaken.

The main speaker is Jesse Jones, president of Computer World Software, of Chicago, who will speak at 10 a.m. on the fair's theme. Jones owns a company that produces a guide for home school teachers on how to access educational resources through the Internet. The name of the book is "Surfing the Home School Network."

The fair begins at 8 a.m. with registration, which is free, and ends at 5 p.m. at the Community Center, 1456 Columbia St. The first session begins at

9 a.m. during which a panel of five parents will describe how they decided to home school their children. Jones will speak at 10 a.m., and representatives from three publishing firms will describe material available to home school parents.

The afternoon session begins at 1 p.m. with a talk by Phyllis Kroning, a local resident, about how she chooses curricula for her six children ages 6 through 15. At 2 p.m. a panel of three parents will explain how they integrate field trips in their home school instruction. At 3 p.m. Phil Night, county association president, will answer questions about the organization and other networking opportunities. A display of home school instructional materials will be in place throughout the day. The fair will end at 5 p.m. Lunch may be purchased in the Community Center Cafeteria for $2.99 for adults and 99 cents for children 12 and under.

No admission will be charged. People with questions should call (000) 000-0000.

✓ Include a headline as part of your advertisement. You also may include an illustration.

✓ Leave at least a half-inch margin on all sides of the 8 1/2- by 11-inch sheet of paper.

✓ Include the time and place of the event. The telephone number also is important.

✓ Write the headline and sketch any illustrations that might be used on the layout. Draw a block(s) to show where the copy or text material will appear. Double space this material on a separate sheet of paper.

✓ After your teacher critiques the ad, make corrections and place a copy in your permanent writing file.

✓ You are not required to use all of the information listed above in the ad.

Note to Teacher:

Encourage the student to present the information as briefly as possible, including program speakers and topics.

A student who has access to a computer should be encouraged to use it. A headline, illustration and copy can be created, especially with a desktop program, in an advertising flier that rivals those produced professionally.

On the Air

Writing a broadcast news script underscores the importance of brevity in communication. For example, a radio newscast may be only a minute long. These broadcasts often summarize the news and read like newspaper headlines. In radio broadcasting, a 60-character, written line represents three seconds of speaking time. It is referred to as "total running time" or TRT. Using this rule of thumb, a one-minute broadcast requires 20 lines of copy. The broadcaster may summarize two or three news stories in such a segment, which limits the amount of detail that can be included.

Guidelines vary from station to station, but a number of generally accepted rules follow:

✓ Write copy on sheets of paper 8 1/2 by 11 inches.

✓ Double space copy in caps and lowercase.

✓ Never divide words from line to line and never break a paragraph from page to page.

✓ Never write more than one story on a page.

✓ Only write on one side of a sheet of paper.

✓ Identify the story by a short line and the date at the top left side of the sheet of paper. Place the TRT at the top right side of the paper.

Example:

House burns   TRT:10
Dec. 22, 0000

Assignment:

1. Prepare a three-minute radio news broadcast based on stories that appear in the current issue of a daily newspaper. You may select one or more stories from each of the following categories: local, state, national and international. Rank these stories according to their news importance or their interest to listeners and present the stories in that order.

A three-minute segment will require 60 lines of copy. Strive to use transitions between news items. Example: Elsewhere in town, the mayor named a police chief. Don't forget to include time and place in each item. Include at least one direct quotation in your newscast. Unless you have recorded your subject's comment, the announcer will have to repeat the words spoken by that person. In such an event, introduce the direct quote in this manner: In Mayor Jill Doe's words: "I selected the best qualified person for the job." Another method: Mayor Jill Doe was quoted as saying: "The best qualified person was selected."

2. After writing the script, practice reading it as though you were a radio announcer. Time your delivery. It may be necessary to add an item or to delete material from your script for the broadcast to match the three-minute mark. Remember, the announcer must hit the mark exactly. After you have perfected your news presentation, deliver it in front of your family. Invite them to watch the clock and to critique your delivery. Did you pronounce names and words correctly? Did the items selected for the broadcast catch and hold the listener's attention?

Note to Teacher:

This assignment offers an excellent excuse for a student to visit a radio and/or television station and to view how scripts are researched, written and staged. If possible, arrange for the student to shadow a news team or someone in the studio for an hour or longer. Encourage the student to inquire about career opportunities during such a visit.

Crossword Capers

The crossword puzzle offers an opportunity to practice one of the briefest forms of communication. No sentences to write. No thoughts to organize. No headlines to create. No information to gather. Just fill in the blanks ACROSS and DOWN by finding synonym substitutes. For beginner or expert, a crossword puzzle may sharpen the mind, encourage keeping pace with world events and build vocabulary.

So, shorten up your writing and sharpen up your mental skills by tackling a crossword puzzle. They make regular appearances in newspapers and magazines. You also can find them on the Internet.

Assignments:

1. Complete as much of a crossword puzzle as possible. Then await the answers, which usually appear the next day in a newspaper. Make a list of the things you learned, including definitions and synonyms, history, people and current events.

2. Construct a crossword puzzle of your own. Draw a rectangle filled with boxes. Set up the ACROSS and DOWN clues, number the boxes and blank out those boxes that are not used. When the assignment is complete, make photo copies and invite members of your family and friends to complete the crossword.

Note to Teacher:

Not all students will be acquainted with the crossword puzzle. You may need to help the student find a puzzle that matches his/her level of expertise. Treat this as an "off the wall" assignment, one designed to explore new writing worlds.

Write It Tight: Lesson 5
Editorial Cartooning

Cartooning offers the author an opportunity to comment on public issues. Look at the editorial section of a newspaper for examples of this art form. The editorial cartoon is linked with the history of newspapering in the Western world and continues to be an integral part of newspaper journalism today, especially in a world that is relying more and more upon visual rather than written expression.

A cartoonist must decide on a focus or thesis statement before the drawing begins. Cartoon objects often are exaggerated. For example, if a public official has large ears, the cartoonist will draw them extra large. Study the ways that cartoonists draw the eyes of their subjects. This exaggeration is a form of ridicule, which is a standard practice in cartooning.

The cartoonist also looks for unusual ways to express an opinion, which may be linked to a recent news development or act by the public official who appears in the cartoon. Each cartoonist develops a style that readers can identify easily.

A cartoon may incorporate words, which often are spoken. Spoken words may appear in balloons in the cartoon or may appear as a cutline beneath the cartoon.

Keep in mind that editorial cartoons are personal expressions of a point of view. They are not intended to be objective or fair to the parties or ideas expressed. They may ridicule, criticize, make fun of public officials, public issues, public proposals. For ethical as well as legal reasons, those individuals who choose to remain private citizens and who are not involved in public issues should not be the subject of editorial cartoons that appear in a newspaper. These cartoons are really figures of speech in visual form. Note that magazine cartoons usually are gag rather than editorial cartoons.

Assignment:

Create an editorial cartoon. First, however, you should study how viewpoints are expressed in cartoons that appear in the editorial section of a newspaper. Before you begin drawing a cartoon, establish a focus or thesis statement that expresses a personal opinion, one that you can defend. Then, use a pencil to sketch the cartoon. When you are satisfied with the results, ink in the sketch and add any words needed to complete the cartoon. Share the cartoon with your teacher and with members of the family. Then place a copy in your permanent writing file.

Note to Teacher:

Art experience or the gift of drawing is not a requirement for this assignment. The major objective is for the student to create a point-of-view statement that can be expressed in cartoon form. Encourage the student to attempt drawing the cartoon. It need not be a work of art. The student may find it difficult, even impossible, to translate that viewpoint into cartoon form. If this mental block occurs, encourage the student to exaggerate, to ridicule. This is uncommon ground for many students, but it is common turf for the cartoonist.

For those students who are acquainted with and have access to a computer drawing program, invite them to create the cartoon by that method.

Complete the Picture

In preparation for the next unit of study in *The Write Stuff Adventure*, we need to know how to write a cutline. The cutline, which is also referred to as a caption, normally appears below a photograph. This information completes the picture story.

You will note in studying cutlines that they are usually one sentence long and identify persons, places and things in the photograph. A single sentence normally accompanies photographs that are used with a story. It may require more than one sentence to complete the story when the photograph does not accompany a story.

Cutlines should appear on a separate sheet of paper, and the copy should be double spaced. Follow these guidelines in writing cutlines:

✓ Use present active verbs to describe action. Present tense enhances immediacy. (Example: John Doe hits a home run to open the sixth inning and the Tigers go on to win, 8-6.)

✓ Identify everyone who is prominent in the photograph by using first and last names.

✓ To be concise, use the phrase: from left. Avoid using the phrase: from left to right. If you are identifying a person in a group, use (left) or whatever word will single out that person. (Example: Jill Doe, left, will be honored at Friday's banquet.)

✓ Avoid telling the reader what is obvious in the photograph. (Example: If the subject is petting a cat, avoid telling your readers that the subject is petting a cat.)

✓ Mention the place the photograph was taken. Sometimes it is important to include the date, especially if the photograph is to be filed in a photo album. Always include cutline information with each photo that appears in an album.

✓ Explain any unusual objects.

Assignment:

Pick three photographs from your personal or family album and write a cutline for each photograph. Include first and last names of people you wish to identify, the event and the date it occurred.

After your teacher critiques the assignment, correct errors and place each cutline with the photograph in the album.

Note to Teacher:

The importance of completing a photo story with cutline information is stressed in the lessons that follow. A student may not appreciate the importance of identifying people by name for the benefit of future generations.

Visual Communication

Lesson 1

The Visual World

Using a camera to capture information, to express ideas and to create artistic compositions is a popular segment in *The Write Stuff Adventure*. For a number of students, this study may culminate the formal study of writing in high school.

While a camera is used, the instructional emphasis is not upon the technical side of picture-taking but upon what we call composition or how objects are arranged in a visual presentation. While some students may receive ribbons and even prize money for photographic prints entered in fairs and other exhibits, the lifetime reward should be the ability to record events for a lively, interesting and documented family photo album. The principles introduced in this study also may be applied to video and to the study of art. Students will learn how to write a cutline and copy blocks to identify photographs. Assignments will also illustrate the importance of words in completing a picture story.

An inexpensive point-and-shoot camera can be used to take pictures assigned in the following lessons. A flash is optional. On the other hand, more sophisticated cameras, lenses and lighting equipment can be used. Parents who are photographers can use these assignments to teach the technical aspects of the craft, including use of a darkroom. For those teachers who have access to a darkroom, black-and-white film can be substituted for the recommended color print film so that students can learn how to develop and print.

In two *Write Stuff* classes, each student shot a 24-exposure roll of ASA 400 Fuji color print film for each assignment, had the film developed and one print made of each negative by commercial photography firms. The student filed the negatives in 8 1/2- by 11-inch film preservers, which can be purchased at a photo supply store. The student's name, date of the assignment and general subject were written at the top of each negative sheet and became a part of the student's permanent writing file.

Assignment: My World

This assignment will introduce you to photography as a visual communication medium. The two or three photographs that you select from your 24 negatives should represent important parts of the world in which you work, study or play. For example, if you enjoy skiing, take your camera along and shoot the slope where you ski, maybe while skiing. If you are a musician, find some way to illustrate your primary interest. For example: the piano keyboard. Examples of other interests include the spokes of a bicycle wheel or a stack of books. It would be possible to include yourself in the photograph by mounting the camera on a tripod and shooting a timed exposure.

✓ Shoot a 24-exposure roll of film. Explore your world and experiment with ways you can show that world.

✓ Turn in at least two but not more than three photographs that best illustrate what you can title "My World" along with cutlines that contain enough information to explain how each photograph illustrates that world. (Review the cutline instructions in your previous lesson.) Your name and the date should appear in the upper left corner of the report and the text of the 25- to 50-word caption should be double spaced. Glue the 3x5 or 4x6 photographs that you select on one page and type the copy on a second page.

✓ Turn in all of your negatives in an 8 1/2 by 11-inch negative protection sheet. A number appears at the bottom of each negative. When you handle negatives, do not touch the image. (Avoid cutting negatives in strips of fewer than four or five frames.) Write your name, the date of the assignment and the subject of your negatives at the top of the protection sheet. Example: John Doe's 5th birthday party. The negatives should appear in the following order as you look at the face of the negative protection sheet:

1 2 3 4 5
6 7 8 9 10
11 etc.

OR

1 2 3 4
5 6 7 8
9 etc.

Note to Teacher:

Because of the delay a student might experience while waiting for negatives and prints to be returned from a commercial photography store, interest can be maintained by having the student begin shooting the next assignment. As soon as negatives and prints are available, the student should be expected to complete the earlier assignment.

Explore ways that a student's best work can be exhibited when the study is completed. This project would be an excellent opportunity for a group of home school teachers to share their photographic skills in teaching students and in arranging an exhibit of their work at a local art gallery, public building or church. On the other hand, a show of an individual student's work can be arranged in the home or in a public location.

The final assignment offers more detailed suggestions about an exhibit, but students should keep track of their three or four favorite negatives and select them for enlargement. Traditionally, a reception is scheduled in conjunction with an exhibit, which is another incentive to encourage the student to participate in *The Write Stuff Adventure* and to reward that effort by sharing the student's success with family and friends.

The Family Album

Most *Write Stuff* students will not choose photography as a career. They will, however, take photographs during their lifetimes and eventually will place them in family albums. Therefore, it is important for a student to follow "good photo habits" by completing the picture story as each photo is placed in the album and by filing negatives.

"I'll remember who those people are in the photograph," the student says as it is arranged in an album.

"But will your grandchildren know?"

"Probably not."

"Then write a cutline that identifies the people and includes the date and place the photograph was taken."

"But that takes too much time."

"Poor excuse for someone who is writing and documenting family history."

Gathering information is an important and essential responsibility of taking pictures whether you're an amateur or a professional. So, continue practicing the information-gathering and writing skills you have acquired through this study.

The question of ethics or good taste arises as you begin to take photographs. Keep in mind that photographs of people clowning around, making funny faces and acting up may be acceptable for inclusion in your family album but might be embarrassing if shown to a different audience. For example, you might photograph your brother making a face, crossing his eyes and pulling on his ears. He knew that you were taking the picture and laughs when he sees it in your family album. It would be in bad taste, however, to enter the photograph in an exhibit without his permission. If he objects, leave the photo in the album. If a photograph may be embarrassing to a member of the family or friend, destroy it as well as the negative. Photographers, as well as writers, should guard against damaging or destroying another person's reputation.

Most of our photography revolves around people pictured in a variety of situations. The lives of people are documented beginning with birth and continuing through death. Some of these photographs are referred to as portraits. The mug shot is a journalistic term that refers to a picture of a person's head and shoulders. People also are documented in static groups and as they relate to one another. This assignment is tailored to introduce you to all of these photographic opportunities.

Assignment:

✓ Shoot a 24-exposure roll of film. Submit all of your negatives, cutlines and the best photos from each of the following:

✓ Take a mug shot, a vertical photograph picturing a person's head and shoulders.

✓ Take a portrait, which traditionally is a vertical photograph of the person's entire body. You may include a prop or two. The portrait often attempts to capture some mood or to suggest a person's personality.

✓ Find four or more volunteers to pose as subjects in a group shot. The traditional approach is to line them up like birds on a fence and shoot them, legs and all. After shooting such a picture, try arranging your group in different ways. Try shooting from different angles, maybe straight on and from a stepladder. Concentrate on faces rather than on legs and limbs. Crop out (eliminate) extraneous matter when framing each picture in the viewfinder. Check background to prevent trees and telephone poles from growing out of heads and to eliminate other distractions, which are referred to as visual static.

✓ Glue your best mug shot and your best portrait on one sheet of paper and several group shots on a second sheet. On a third sheet type cutlines for each photograph in which you note the place, date and identify each person by full name, from left.

✓ Discuss this assignment with your teacher. Explain what you most liked about it and what created problems for you.

Visual Communication: Lesson 3

The Picture Story

Many photo albums are filled with pictures showing people who were lined up against a brick wall or with some other distraction in the background. Also common are pictures in which the person is shown head-to-toe surrounded by objects that distract rather than help tell a story. The idea of shooting up close as well as from a distance apparently never crosses the photographer's mind.

At least two practices contribute to this problem: 1) only one frame (negative, shot) was taken of the subject and 2) only one viewpoint was sought. Note that you are assigned to take a 24-exposure roll of each assignment. The objective is not to waste film but to increase the options the photographer has in selecting suitable prints for an album, an exhibit or a picture story.

In the lesson that follows, you will be assigned to select a subject and to take a series of photographs of that subject from various vantage points. For example, the subject could be an individual, a chair, a car, a bicycle. This lesson illustrates the importance of capturing a variety of photographic images that may be used together or separately to tell a story. For example: If a photographer were taking pictures of a toy collection, he would take several pictures of the entire collection, including the room or setting where the collection is housed. The photographer then would move closer and take pictures of part of the collection from various camera angles and finally move in and take closeups of single toy or even a part of a toy from different angles.

Assignment:

✓ Select a single subject and shoot a variety of pictures at different distances from the subject. Example: Photographs taken 15 feet, 10 feet and 5 or fewer feet from the subject. Shoot a 24-exposure roll of film for this assignment and practice taking vertical and horizontal photographs, which will offer an editor choices in laying out (arranging) pictures with headlines, cutlines and text.

✓ Turn in your negatives and a variety of prints that tell a story. This selection should include photos taken at different distances from the subject, including a close-up. Remember to write your name and the date you shot the assignment on the negative holder.

✓ Write a 50-word report in which you summarize the subject and identify the objects in the photographs. Remember to include your name and the date in the top left corner of the page and double space your report. Mount the photographs on a separate sheet of paper.

✓ Discuss this assignment with your teacher.

Note to Teacher:

Students will learn, often through experimentation, that they can get only so close to a subject with a point-and-shoot camera because of the way the lens is designed. For example, the minimum distance may be 4 to 6 feet. Those students who have wide-angle, micro and telephoto lenses will be able to narrow the distance between the subject and camera.

As we will learn in our study of composition, it is unnecessary to take "the whole thing" when shooting an object. For example, when a part of an object has been omitted from the picture, the eye of the viewer will complete the picture in his/her mind. Students should be encouraged to crop (eliminate) portions of an object when taking photographs. For example, in this assignment, the student should take several pictures of an object so close that only portions of the object appear. Another example: a horizontal picture of a person showing the face from below the jaw to just above the eyebrows. Encourage the student to eliminate as much of any distracting background as possible. For those students who have more sophisticated cameras, background can be eliminated by narrowing the depth of field.

Principles of Composition

Principles of composition apply to all visual presentations, including the work of artists and photographers. By composition, we refer to the arrangement of various elements in a painting, on a printed page, on the television screen, in a photograph.

In this lesson, you are encouraged to become acquainted with the following principles:

✓ A strong center of interest should be present in a photograph. The photographer should have some idea about the focus or thesis statement he/she wishes to make before snapping the camera's shutter. Otherwise, the photograph may fail to catch the viewer's eye in much the same way as an unfocused essay, feature article, news story or advertisement will fail to catch the reader's attention.

✓ The horizon line should not fall in the middle of a photograph. In other words, where the ocean meets the sky should not appear in the center of the photograph.

✓ Don't aim for the bull's eye when shooting a picture. A subject that appears dead-center in your photograph often fails to create the discord needed to attract and to hold the viewer's attention. (A head-and-shoulders photograph of a person, which is referred to as a mug shot, is an exception to this rule.)

✓ When taking pictures of broad vistas like oceans, mountains and landscapes, try to frame a portion of the view by including part of a tree or some other nearby object at the top or at the side of the photograph. This "framing" will add a dimension to your photograph.

✓ Include leading lines, shapes and forms in your photographs. For example, a line can be used to lead the viewer's eye to the subject. Shapes that may make a composition pleasing to the eye include the L, T, C, X, plus signs and curves.

✓ The rule of thirds is a basic principle of composition that suggests placing the subject at one or more of four lines that intersect a photograph. (An example appears at the end of the chapter.)

Assignment

✓ You are assigned to shoot a 24-exposure roll of film. Shoot several different frames to illustrate principles of composition as follows:

1) Take photographs of a landscape in which the horizon line appears at different positions in at least three frames, including a dead-center shot.

2) To illustrate the bull's-eye principle, take photographs of a subject that appears in the center of your photograph and then appears off-center in one or two other frames.

3) Take pictures of a landscape that is framed on the top or side by some object like a tree.

4) Take a picture of a landscape in which a roadway, sidewalk, fence or some object establishes a line in the foreground that leads the eye to a building or to some other object.

5) Take one or more pictures of an object that suggests motion. Examples: the curved trunk of an elephant, a large X drawn on a blackboard, a T-shaped clothes-line support, an L-shaped piece of equipment like a square used by carpenters.

6) Take a photograph that illustrates the "rule of thirds" principle of composition.

✓ Glue each example on an 8 1/2- by 11-inch sheet of paper accompanied by a written explanation of each example.

✓ Turn in the examples and your negatives to your teacher and be prepared to discuss this assignment with your teacher.

Note to Teacher:

Encourage your student to explain how his/her photographs illustrate the basic principles of composition studied in this lesson. Note, too, that the student has been assigned to violate two principles by shooting the horizon line in the middle of one photograph and by shooting a subject dead-center in another.

Make certain that the student is filing negatives correctly and is preserving them in a notebook or in some other manner.

Photo Credit: Dean Rea

The Feature

In this assignment the photographer can select a subject and shoot it in any manner that he/she chooses. For example: You might take pictures of someone's birthday. Begin shooting when the party begins and continue taking pictures when gifts are opened, candles are blown out, ice cream and cake are eaten and games are played. Include pictures of the guests and a few close-up photographs.

Any subject may serve as a photographic feature, including a family picnic, a parade, a day at the beach, a rodeo, a fishing trip, a church outing, children flying kites, a track and field meet, a baseball game. Keep in mind that you should take photographs that reflect the focus or theme of the feature.

It is possible to shoot a photo feature that is self-explanatory. Normally, however, cutlines and a short article will be needed to complete the picture story. Avoid repeating information and be prepared to select one photograph that would dominate or be the largest element if the feature were to appear in some publication.

A number of home school students may have an opportunity to help produce yearbooks for various organizations. Think of each page in the yearbook as a layout. If you were the editor, how would you arrange the elements in this assignment on a page?

Assignment: The Feature

✓ Shoot a 24-exposure roll of film.

✓ Select three or four photographs that best illustrate the activity you have recorded on film. Designate the photograph that you believe should dominate (be the largest) in a layout.

✓ Write a cutline for each of the three or four photographs you have selected.

✓ Write a 100-word copy block to accompany the photographs. This information should complete the story that is not told in the photographs and cutlines.

✓ Turn in the assignment and discuss it with your teacher. Correct the copy block and place this project in your permanent writing file.

Note to Teacher:

You may want to take this assignment one more step and have the student prepare a page layout for a fictional yearbook. Use an 8 1/2- by 11-inch page size and have the student pencil in the photographs, cutlines, a headline and copy (text) block. The photographs may be enlarged or reduced to match the space outlined on the page. The sizes of the layout elements will be approximate unless the student has access to a desktop publishing program and a scanner to transfer the photo images from negatives to computer screen.

Layout guidelines include the following:

✓ Do not separate the headline and copy block with a photograph or artwork.
✓ Align layout elements vertically and horizontally in such a way that white space is not trapped on all four sides.
✓ Photographs may be cropped but should not be mortised by removing sections or by cutting photographs into odd shapes. Normally, photographs should be treated as vertical or horizontal images. Avoid cropping them into squares.

The Workplace

This photographic assignment deals with one of the most interesting areas of photography: the portrait that reflects the occupation, interest or background of your subject.

Examples include an artist painting a picture, a carpenter constructing a building, a gardener at work, a hobbyist flying a model airplane, an angler fishing, a youngster playing a sport, a farmer harvesting a crop.

Because it is a portrait, you will need the subject's cooperation. Therefore, you will need to discuss the photograph with your subject in advance and to make certain that you have the proper setting, tools, etc. It is permissible for you, the photographer, to pose your subject so that you can tell the story properly with a single photograph.

Even though you may not expect to sell or to place this photograph in an exhibit, you will be assigned to obtain a signed model release from your subject. A copy appears at the end of this assignment. A person owns the property rights to his or her photographic likeness except when that person is photographed during a public event. For example, permission is not required if the subject appears in a news or feature photo that is published in a newspaper or is shown during a television newscast.

If the event is not public, photographers routinely obtain signed model release forms from their subjects. People who are called models often are paid for appearing in photographs. In this assignment, you are to select a subject other than a family member. Make certain that your subject understands that you are required to obtain a signed model release form as part of your assignment.

Assignment: The Workplace

✓ Select a subject other than a member of your family and make arrangements to interview and to photograph that person in the workplace. Obtain a signed model release form and verbal permission to write and publish an article about that person. It is important that you study and understand what's in this release form so you can explain it to your subject. Make several photocopies of the release form and place them in your photo equipment bag for future use.

✓ Shoot a 24-exposure roll. That's correct, all 24 exposures in a roll, which will give you an opportunity to shoot from different angles and even to shoot the subject in different areas of the workplace. You are to select and turn in only ONE photograph, all of your negatives and the signed model release form.

✓ Write and turn in a cutline and a 250-word article about your subject to accompany the photograph. Prepare for an interview as well as for photographing the subject. Take the photographs first and then conduct the interview. This will help you establish rapport with the respondent.

✓ Discuss the assignment with your teacher. Revise your article based on your teacher's critique. Place one copy of the assignment in your permanent writing file and forward a copy, including a photograph, to your subject with a thank-you note.

Note to Teacher:

The examples suggest that the workplace is a broad term and can apply to most any person and activity. The assignment is designed to move the student out of his/her comfort zone and to help him/her to grow socially as well as as a writer and photographer.

In shooting this assignment, the student should move the subject as close to the work activity as possible. The student is encouraged to photograph the subject from various distances and from various angles. Keep in mind that the student is to select only one photograph. Require the student to make the selection without your help. You can ask the student about that choice during the critiquing session.

Encourage the student to pick a person who may have an interesting occupation or hobby. Your neighborhood newspaper, especially a weekly, may be interested in publishing the photograph and the story.

Signed release forms should be obtained for photographs that are intended to be displayed in public, including exhibits and entries in photo contests. A signed release should also be obtained from anyone who appears in a photograph that is intended for sale or for use in an advertisement or promotional brochure.

(The model release form appears on the next page.)

MODEL RELEASE

I hereby authorize photographer Dean Rea and/or parties designated by the photographer, including clients, purchasers, agencies and periodicals or other printed matter and their editors, to use my photograph in conjunction with my name or a fictitious name for sale to or reproduction in any medium the photographer or photographer's designee sees fit for purposes of advertising, display, exhibition or editorial use.

I affirm that I am of legal age (18 years or older).

Date: _____

Signature: _____

Witnessed by: _____

GUARDIAN'S CONSENT

I am the parent or guardian of _____

I have read and hereby approve the attached MODEL RELEASE and consent to the photographer's use subject to the terms mentioned therein.

I affirm that I have the legal right to issue such consent.

Date: _____

Signature: _____

Visual Communication: Lesson 7
Pretty Pictures

This assignment gives you full rein to take pretty pictures of outdoor scenery from close up and from a distance. These photographs often are referred to as "artsy shots." They open creative vistas that often challenge and reward the photographer with his/her favorite work.

This assignment offers you an opportunity to shoot something of your choice, maybe while on a field trip or in your backyard. Explore different lighting opportunities. Notice how light reflects, often brilliantly, off water. Take pictures of patterns in the sand, the texture of leaves, the contrast of colors. Try your hand at back lighting a subject by placing the light source (usually the sun) behind your subject. A halo effect often occurs around your subject. When documenting patterns and textures, move as close to the subject as possible. For example, move the camera directly above patterns in the sand created by wind and waves or above a leaf to show its texture.

Your viewfinder also should allow you to take a look at outdoor scenery on a grand scale: mountains, valleys, forests, the ocean. The only people who appear in these photographs should be those you use for scale or for human interest. If you have a telephoto lens, use it.

Remember, the focus is upon scenery, not people.

Assignment: Pretty Pictures

✓ Shoot a 24-exposure roll of film.

✓ Turn in all of your negatives and your best four to six prints accompanied by cut-lines that include the date and the place.

✓ Discuss the assignment with your teacher and explain why you selected these prints.

Note to Teacher:

Students often will select one or more prints from this assignment for inclusion in a photo exhibit, which is discussed in the next lesson.

Students who exhibit a strong interest in photography should be encouraged to continue shooting for a family album. They also should begin creating photographic "essays" that examine themes in detail. For example, a portfolio (or file) of photographs might deal with children at play, antiquated farm machinery, farm life, architecture, seascapes.

Photographic histories are available through many resources. The serious student of photography should read about and view the work of Ansel Adams, Timothy O'Sullivan, Jacob Riis, Cornell Capa, Margaret Bourke-White, Dorthea Lange, Brian Lanker, Lewis Hine, Edward Weston, Eddie Adams, Minor White and Henri Cartier-Bresson. The work of more current photographic giants may be viewed in such publications as the National Geographic and even on the Internet.

Community colleges often offer photographic technique courses that include darkroom experience through extension programs. In some cases, high school students may be accepted. Local arts groups and studios also may offer similar instructional opportunities.

The Photo Exhibit

Note to Teacher:

A photo exhibit is the traditional method of showing a student's work and is popular with students, parents and friends. The suggestion to stage an exhibit came from my daughter who was an art education major in college. I was teaching an introductory class at Biola University near Los Angeles and told my daughter about the outstanding black-and-white photographs that students were shooting and developing in the lab.

"Do an exhibit," she said.

"But do you know the incredible amount of work involved in arranging such a show?"

"Sure," she said, "but photographers are artists, and you need to acknowledge their accomplishments by sharing their work with other people."

So, a lot of hard work led to the setting up of panels and mounting the photos of more than 30 students in the university cafeteria. I later repeated the process while acquainting two home school writing classes with photography and composition.

The Write Stuff Adventure has promoted publication of students' work beginning with their first efforts, which may end up on a refrigerator, to publication of stories in newspapers and magazines. The photo exhibit publicly acknowledges the importance of visual expression and provides an incentive for students to strive for excellence.

If the exhibit is of a single student's work, six to eight photographs should be displayed. If the exhibit is the work of several students, three enlarged prints each is a good number. Select an art gallery or some place that is well lit.

Prints of two of my home school classes were displayed for a month at a local art gallery. When the exhibit opened, a reception was arranged by parents on a Saturday afternoon. Punch and cookies were served and many family members and friends attended.

Students were instructed to select their three favorite negatives. One negative was enlarged to 11 by 14 inches and the other two to 5 by 7 inches. Mounting boards with 2-inch margins (13 by 16 and 7 by 9) were purchased and cut to size at a print shop. Students then learned how to mount their glossy print enlargements on the commercial cardboard, using a photo mount spray adhesive. This normally was done in my garage during the final meeting of the class, which gave us an opportunity to celebrate with refreshments.

Another popular prelude to the exhibit was taking a group shot of the students, who arranged themselves around playground equipment, ladders and other props while insisting that I "shoot a whole 24-exposure roll." The favorite negative was enlarged to 11 by 14 inches. The print and a copy block describing the class and identifying the students were mounted on a piece of commercial cardboard for use in introducing the exhibit.

In putting up the display, the bottom of each 11- by 14-inch enlargement sat on an imaginary line so that the print was slightly above eye-level. The two 5- by 7-inch enlargements and a card bearing the name of the photographer were arranged below.

The single student exhibit should also include a reception. Churches, banks, restaurants and public libraries often make space available for such exhibits.

It is important, however, to arrange exhibits several months, even a year, in advance. Therefore, if a home school study group embarks upon this project, someone should be assigned to line up a gallery before the instruction begins. A group study needs to be led by a teacher or by a resource person who is acquainted with photography and with the principles of composition. The work of a dozen students can be critiqued weekly in an hour or two. (I always invited parents to sit in on such classes if they wished. Several were interested in learning more about photography.)

For those of you who wish to extend this instruction, assign the student to take pictures using a video camera. Instruct the student 1) to follow the rules of composition he/she has learned in this class, 2) to create meaningful verbal cutlines to complete each picture story and 3) to be selective in filming family and other events. The latter practice is important so that family and friends do not have to sit through "a lot of boring stuff" when the video is replayed. If your family has access to video editing equipment, assign that task to the student and arrange a showing for family and friends. For those students who are computer experts, encourage them to set up photo home pages on the Internet and to change them periodically.

Writing the Short Story

Note to Teacher

Many students want to be creative writers. They envision freedom to soar with eagles, to be published, to be rich and famous. Such dreams quickly crumble when they discover that creative writing is highly structured, especially a short story. The serious student, however, will warm to the challenge of creating characters, mapping scenes and sequels, charting ways for the hero to scale seemingly insurmountable obstacles until the journey ends.

For me, a home school teacher, I faced the daunting task of teaching short story writing because fiction was a stranger in my writing stable. Meanwhile, a dozen of my students who had spent two years writing non-fiction were ready to tackle the short story. I needed the help of a how-to source. So, I searched for and discovered a book, *Writing the Short Story: A Hands-On Program*, published by Writer's Digest Books. The author, Jack M. Bickham, of Norman, Oklahoma, was a former creative writing professor who had published more than 80 novels. As I read the book it became apparent that Bickham had not only mastered the subject, but had also presented it in short, understandable bites that a beginner of any age could digest.

I assigned students to read and complete the assignments outlined in the book. The first short story of 2,000 to 3,000 words was assigned during the seventh week and was due two weeks later. The stories then were critiqued and revised by students following Bickham's guidelines. Granted, I included commentary and instruction during the lecture sessions, but the major focus rested on Bickham's book.

For those people who want to teach short story writing by using this book, the following suggestions are offered:

First Three-Month Study Period:

Lesson 1:

Read Chapters 1 and 2. As you read Chapter 3, "Taking Inventory," complete the self-inventory cards and more inventory on page 14. Read the first three chapter entries in the appendix.

Lesson 2:

Read Chapter 4 and its appendix section. Complete the appealing traits assignment on page 21, negative traits assignment on page 23 and the tags assignment on page 25.

Lesson 3:

Read the "The Architecture of Story" section, Chapter 5 and its appendix section. Complete the three-card conflict assignment on page 43, the decision assignment on pages 44-45 and the characters assignment on pages 49-50.

Lesson 4:

Read Chapters 6 and 7 and their appendix sections. Complete the six-card assignment on page 70. Begin the real people assignment on pages 55-56 and prepare the dialogue card assignment on pages 57-58.

Lesson 5:

Read the "What Makes People Tick" section, Chapters 8 and 9 and their appendix sections.

Lesson 6:

Read "The Beauty—and Utility—of Sacrifice" section, Chapters 10 and 11 and their appendix sections. Continue building your character trait card file, establish your story question and use cards to plan scenes and sequences.

Lesson 7:

Read Chapters 12, 13 and 14 and their appendix sections. The first draft of a 2,000- to 3,000-word short story is due in two weeks. A first-person protagonist's viewpoint should not be used in telling this story.

Lesson 8:

Discuss the short story that is being written.

Lesson 9:

The first draft is due.

Lesson 10:

Read the "Devices: Flashback, Dialogue, Voice" section, Chapter 15 and its appendix section. Complete the first revision of your short story.

Lesson 11:

Read Chapters 16, 17 and 18 and their appendix sections. Turn in the final draft of your short story.

Second Three-Month Study Period:

Assign two short stories during this study. The student should follow much the same map in creating these stories, including rewriting. The student should be required to use a first-person protagonist's viewpoint in one of the stories.

Note to Teachers:

It is imperative that the student keep pace with Bickham's assignments, especially card-building tasks. Your role may be largely an administrative one as the student moves through the textbook. The same imperative applies during the second three-month study. Encourage the student to establish a specific time, place and duration for working. Follow the textbook author's advice, which is described in Chapter 3.

An Additional Resource:

Another excellent how-to book, *Writing to Sell*, has been published by Writer's Digest Book. The author, Scott Meredith, was regarded as one of the most successful literary agents before his death in 1993. The student may wish to read through this resource while writing the second and third short stories.

When this study is completed, don't be surprised if your student suggests that he/she continue this adventure by writing a novel.

"Can't be done," the skeptic says.

"Can too," the optimist replies.

"How?"

"One page a day for a year."

"But then who will publish your book?"

"Ah, now that's another adventure...."

---

2. Merideth, Scott. "Writing to Sell," Fourth Edition, Cincinnati, Ohio, F&W Publications, 1995.